Stand Out

Grammar Challenge

THOMSON

HEINLE

Australia • Canada • Mexico • Singapore • Spain • United Kingdom • United States

THOMSON
™
HEINLE

Stand Out 3
Grammar Challenge

Acquisitions Editor: *Sherrise Roehr*

Managing Editor: *James W. Brown*

Developmental Editors: *Ingrid Wisniewska, Jill Korey O'Sullivan*

Associate Developmental Editor: *Sarah Barnicle*

Editorial Assistant: *Elizabeth Allen*

Marketing Manager: *Eric Bredenberg*

Director, Global ESL Training & Development: *Evelyn Nelson*

Production Editor: *Jeff Freeland*

Senior Manufacturing Coordinator: *Mary Beth Hennebury*

Compositor: *A Plus Publishing Services*

Contributing Writer: *John Chapman*

Printer: *Patterson Printing*

Printed in the United States of America.

 7 8 9 10   06 05

For more information, contact Heinle, 25 Thomson Place, Boston, MA 02210 USA,
or you can visit our Internet site at http://www.heinle.com

For permission to use material from this text or product, contact us:

Tel	1-800-730-2214
Fax	1-800-730-2215
Web	www.thomsonrights.com

ISBN: 0-8384-3938-1

TO THE TEACHER

Stand Out Grammar Challenge 3 challenges students to develop and expand their grammar skills through sixty-four guided exercises or "challenges."

Each Challenge includes:

▶ **Charts** Clear grammar charts help the teacher lay out the structure's components and provide useful example sentences.

▶ **Notes** Notes within the charts help students understand important shifts in language use and meaning through concise explanations.

▶ **Practice** Exercises challenge students to master grammar structures while reviewing the vocabulary and thematic contexts actively taught in *Stand Out Student Book 3*. Additional exercises reinforce grammar structures passively introduced in *Stand Out Student Book 3* contexts.

How to use the *Stand Out Grammar Challenge 3* workbook

The *Stand Out Grammar Challenge 3* workbook can be used in a variety of ways:

- The grammar challenges can be assigned daily or on an as-needed basis.

- The grammar challenges can be completed individually, with a partner, or as a class.

- Students may complete challenges at home or in the classroom.

- Instructors can provide guided feedback upon completion, or ask students to self-correct or peer-edit. All exercises are formatted to provide for ease of correction and assessment.

- The *Grammar Challenge 3* answer key is available to teachers on the *Stand Out* web site at: **standout.heinle.com** It can be printed out for student use.

- The grammar challenges need not be followed in any particular order within a unit. Some challenges will be review for students, while others will reinforce the newer structures from *Stand Out Student Book 3*.

- The *Stand Out Grammar Challenge 3* workbook is an effective supplement in a multi-level classroom because it challenges the highly motivated students while providing support for students who need extra reinforcement.

The appendix includes a glossary of grammar terms with examples. This is intended as a reference for students and teachers, but it is not intended that all these terms will be understood at this level. The appendix also includes grammar charts from the *Stand Out Student Book 3* appendix as well as lists of irregular verbs and verb conjugations.

However you choose to use it, you'll find that the *Stand Out Grammar Challenge 3* workbook is a flexible and effective grammar tool for teachers and students seeking challenging grammar instruction.

CONTENTS

UNIT 1 Balancing Your Life

CHALLENGE 1 ▶ Adverbs of frequency

Frequency word	Frequency	Example
always	100%	I **always** go running on Saturday morning.
usually	⇩	You **usually** join me at 8:00.
often	⇩	We were **often** tired after we ran.
sometimes	⇩	He **sometimes** had breakfast with friends.
rarely/seldom	⇩	She **seldom** runs in the winter.
never	0%	They **never** run in the snow.

- Frequency words come after the verb **be** but before other main verbs.
- **Usually, often,** and **sometimes** can come at the beginning of a sentence.

A Choose the correct adverb. Fill in the bubble completely.

EXAMPLE: I am never late to school. I am _____ on time.   ○ seldom ● always

1. I usually go to the library to study. I _____ study at home.   ○ often ○ rarely
2. Every Saturday and Sunday I sleep late. I _____ sleep late on weekends.   ○ never ○ always
3. Michel seldom gets enough time to study. He almost _____ needs more time.   ○ always ○ never
4. Luisa rarely organizes her work. She is _____ disorganized.   ○ seldom ○ usually
5. We always try to be quiet. We _____ disturb others.   ○ always ○ rarely
6. Good study habits are often beneficial. They _____ make learning easier.   ○ never ○ usually

B Write about Michel. Place the adverbs in the sentences.

EXAMPLE: accomplishes everything that needs to get done (usually)
    **He usually accomplishes everything that needs to get done.**

1. was very busy in the morning (always)

    _____

2. kept people waiting (sometimes)

    _____

3. got a chance to take a break (never)

    _____

4. eats lunch in the office (often)

    _____

5. finds time to relax (rarely)

    _____

6. is tired at the end of the day (usually)

    _____

7. thinks about work after 5:00 P.M. (seldom)

    _____

8. makes time for his family (always)

    _____

CHALLENGE 2 ▶ Questions with *What time* and *How often*

What time . . . How often . . .	*do/does/* *did/will*	Subject	Base verb	Complement	Short answer
What time **What time**	will does	you it	leave start?	home?	At 8:00 A.M. Right after school.
How often **How often**	do did	they she	go go	to the movies? with them?	Every Saturday. Once a month.

- **What time** questions ask about an exact time.
- **How often** questions ask how many times something happens. The answers contain a frequency expression such as **every morning, once a week, twice a month, three times a year,** and **from time to time.**

A Complete the questions. Use *When* or *How often*.

EXAMPLE: Q: _____**How often**_____ do you clean the house?   A: Once a week.

1. Q: _____ does he get up on Saturday?   A: At 9:00 A.M.
2. Q: _____ does he brush his teeth?   A: Twice a day.
3. Q: _____ do you see the doctor?   A: Once a year.
4. Q: _____ does she read in bed?   A: Every night.
5. Q: _____ will you change your clothes?   A: After work.
6. Q: _____ did you take a walk?   A: At noon.

B Read the answers, then write the questions. Change verb tenses as needed.

EXAMPLE: Q: (Grandpa / see his grandchildren)
        _____*How often does Grandpa see his grandchildren?*_____
        A: Once a week.

1. Q: (you / will have a day off)
   _____
   A: Once a month.
2. Q: (Lydia / go running)
   _____
   A: Every day.
3. Q: (Alex / went to bed)
   _____
   A: At midnight.
4. Q: (your sister / practice piano)
   _____
   A: Before she goes to bed.

5. Q: (your friends / finish work)
   _____
   A: At 6:00 P.M.
6. Q: (you / spend time alone)
   _____
   A: From time to time.
7. Q: (you / will do yoga)
   _____
   A: Every morning.
8. Q: (your uncle / visit you)
   _____
   A: Twice a year.

UNIT 1 — Balancing Your Life

CHALLENGE 3 ▸ *Can*

Statement	Question	Explanation
He **can** (**can't**) swim.	**Can** she speak Chinese?	Ability
You **can** walk or drive to work.	**Can** we take a train to Tokyo?	Possibility
Children **can't** buy cigarettes.	**Can** I borrow your car?	Permission
	Can you repeat that, please?	Polite request

• The negative of **can** is **cannot.** The contraction is **can't.**

A Write sentences with *can* using the words given.

EXAMPLE: (Question: you / turn off the TV)
            ___*Can you turn off the TV?*_____

1. (Question: we / see the apartment this afternoon)

    _____

2. (Question: you / buy me a cup of coffee)

    _____

3. (Negative statement: she / pay $1000 a month rent)

    _____

4. (Question: you / spell your last name)

    _____

5. (Question: I / please use your phone)

    _____

6. (Statement: she / help you later)

    _____

7. (Question: they / understand the lesson)

    _____

8. (Negative statement: you / take my dictionary home)

    _____

B Match each statement in A with the correct explanation from the chart.

EXAMPLE: ___*polite request*_____

1. _____   5. _____
2. _____   6. _____
3. _____   7. _____
4. _____   8. _____

Will and be going to

CHALLENGE 4 ▶ *Will* and *be going to*

Will	Be going to	Use
You'**ll** love your new job. It **will** be interesting.	You'**re going to** like your boss.	Prediction
Monday **will** be your first day.	—	Scheduled event
I'**ll** help you move your things.	—	Offer to help
—	I'**m going to** change jobs, too.	Plan
I'**ll** call you Monday morning. I **won't** forget.	—	Promise

• The contraction of **will** is '**ll**. The negative form of **will** is **will not** or **won't**.

A **Match each statement with the correct use from the chart.**

EXAMPLE: Franco's going to go shopping this afternoon. __*plan*_____

1. The mall will open at 9:00.   _____

2. It will be crowded.   _____

3. I won't tell you what to buy.   _____

4. I'll help you carry your bags.   _____

5. We're going to go home at 2:00.   _____

6. You're going to be tired.   _____

B **Choose *will* or *be going to* and use the words in parentheses to write sentences.**

EXAMPLE: (promise) take care of the children Saturday night
           __*I'll take care of the children Saturday night.*_____

1. (plan) we / have six children

    _____

2. (offer to help) I / help with the housework

    _____

3. (promise) I / be there / when you need me

    _____

4. (scheduled event) the babysitter / arrive at 8:00 P.M.

    _____

5. (prediction) we / have fun raising our kids

    _____

6. (plan) we / save money for a new car

    _____

7. (prediction) you / love being a father

    _____

8. (scheduled event) our oldest child / start school / next year

    _____

9. (promise) I / be home early

    _____

10. (offer to help) I / put the kids to sleep

    _____

Balancing Your Life

CHALLENGE 5 ▶ Adverbial clauses with *because* and *so (that)*

Main clause	*Because / So that*	Adverbial clause
Zhou took an ESL course	**because**	he needed English for his job.
He went to night school	**because**	he works during the day.
Zhou's mother is coming	**so (that)**	she can take care of the twins.
They are looking for a bigger house	**so (that)**	they will have room for everyone.

• Adverbial clauses with **because** give reasons why. Clauses with **so** or **so that** give purposes.

A **Write the correct word to complete each sentence.**

EXAMPLE: Tuba wants to get a job _____*so that*_____ she can help her husband.

   Tuba can't get a job now (1) _____ she has children at home. She can get a job next year
(2) _____ the children will be in school. She is studying computers (3) _____
she can get a good job.

   Lam can't send his grandchildren to college (4) _____ it is too expensive. He is thinking
about borrowing money (5) _____ they can attend. His grandchildren may get jobs
(6) _____ they can help pay for college.

B **Use an item from each column to write sentences with *because* and *so* about Luisa.**

~~Luisa leaves the house at 8:30~~	she would not get cold
she takes the bus	she would get to work early
she wore a coat	it's cheaper than a taxi
she didn't take an umbrella	~~she gets to work at 9:00~~
her daughter stayed home	it wasn't raining
today she left home at 8:00	she was sick

EXAMPLE: *Luisa leaves the house at 8:30 so she gets to work at 9:00.* _____

1. _____

2. _____

3. _____

4. _____

5. _____

Balancing Your Life

CHALLENGE 6 ▸ *When* clauses

Time period	Main clause	*When* clause
Past	My sister **had** her first child	**when** she was 22 years old.
Present	Her children **do** their homework	**when** they get home from school.
Future	She **will get** a job outside the house	**when** the children are older.

- The verbs in both clauses of a past or present sentence are in the same tense.
- A **when** clause in the simple present describes a truth, a habit, or a general rule.
- In a future sentence, use the future tense in the main clause, and the present tense in the **when** clause.
- If the **when** clause comes before the main clause, use a comma (,).

A Complete the sentences. Use the correct tense of a verb from the box.

EXAMPLE: My in-laws take care of the children when my wife and I _____***are***_____ at work.

1. We _____ dinner together when we get home.
2. When we finish eating, we all _____ the dishes.
3. Tomorrow you will watch the game when you _____ home from work.
4. The children like to hear stories when I _____ them to bed.
5. My wife _____ to them when she puts them to bed.
6. Some little children _____ when their parents put them to bed.
7. When we save enough money, we _____ a new car.
8. We will use the car when we _____ a vacation.

> put
> have
> wash
> buy
> get
> b̶e̶
> take
> cry
> sing

B Use the words to write a sentence that begins with a *when* clause. Change the verbs to the correct tense.

EXAMPLE: Future: (my stepson / travel / to Spain / when / he / finish / college)
   ___***When he finishes college, my stepson will travel to Spain.***___

1. Past: (my grandfather / live with us / when / I / be / young)

   _____

2. Future: (my cousin / live with us / when / she / come / to this country)

   _____

3. Present: (people / feel / comfortable / when / they / live / with family members)

   _____

4. Past: (my grandfather / die / when / he / be / 80 years old)

   _____

5. Past: (I / not like / my job / when / I / start / it)

   _____

6. Future: (I / stop working / when / I / be / 60 years old)

   _____

Balancing Your Life

CHALLENGE 7 ▶ Questions and short answers with *when* clauses

Time	Main clause	*When* clause	Short answer	
Present	**Are** you usually happy	when you get to work?	Yes, I **am**.	No, I**'m** not.
Present	**Does** she have coffee	when she gets to work?	Yes, she **does**.	No, she **doesn't**.
Past	**Did** you talk to the boss	when you got to work?	Yes, I **did**.	No, I **didn't**.
Future	**Will** you get a better job	when you leave this one?	Yes, I **will**.	No, I **won't**.

• In short answers, use the same tense as the main clause of the question.

A Circle the correct words.

EXAMPLE: Did your brother take a break when he (is /(was)) tired? Yes, he ((did)/ was).

1. (Does / Did) he go to the library when he needed to do research? Yes, he (does / did).
2. When he (is / was) busy, does he take time to relax? No, he (doesn't / didn't).
3. (Do / Did) your friends have pizza when they left the library? Yes, they (do / did).
4. (Are / Will) they study when exams are over? No, they (aren't / won't).
5. When they (go / will go) home, will they watch TV? Yes, they (do / will).
6. Is your friend nervous when he (takes / will take) exams? No, he (isn't / won't).
7. (Do / Did) he study a lot when he was on vacation? Yes, he (did / was).
8. When you (see / saw) him, was he happy? Yes, he (is / was).

B Use information in the chart to write questions and short answers.

Who	When	What	Yes	No
your friends	(present)	EXAMPLE: watch TV / study	X	
your sister	(present)	1. use a dictionary / not know a word	X	
you	(future)	2. take more math / finish this course		X
your coworkers	(past)	3. study Spanish / be in high school	X	
you	(present)	4. stay up all night / have a test		X
your aunt	(future)	5. buy a new computer / finish college	X	
your father	(past)	6. study languages / be in high school		X

EXAMPLE: ___*Do your friends watch TV when they study?*___   ___*Yes, they do.*___

1. _____   _____
2. _____   _____
3. _____   _____
4. _____   _____
5. _____   _____
6. _____   _____

Balancing Your Life

CHALLENGE 8 ▸ Gerunds as subjects

Gerund as subject	Verb	Complement
Reading	improves	the mind.
Learning new skills	is	exciting.
Not spending time with your family	creates	problems.
Taking regular vacations	is	good for you.

- A gerund can be used as the subject of a sentence.
- A gerund can be part of a phrase.
- Use **not** in front of a gerund to make it negative.
- A gerund is followed by a singular verb even if it contains a plural noun.

A Complete each sentence using a gerund as the subject.

EXAMPLE: It isn't fair to copy assignments.   ___*Copying assignments*___ isn't fair.

1. It is fun to learn a language.   _____ is fun.
2. It is difficult to study with distractions.   _____ is difficult.
3. It causes problems if you don't study.   _____ causes problems.
4. It isn't always fun to do homework.   _____ isn't always fun.
5. It takes time to go over assignments.   _____ takes time.

B Use a gerund subject and a present tense verb to complete each sentence.

Gerund subjects	Verbs
~~talking~~	mean
taking	cause
learning	~~help~~
spending	create
reading	take
getting	be
saving	improve

EXAMPLE: _____*Talking*_____ with friends _____*helps*_____ people make good decisions.

1. _____ a good education _____ you will make more money.
2. _____ time with friends _____ relaxing.
3. Not _____ enough money _____ problems in later life.
4. _____ vitamins _____ health.
5. Not _____ instructions _____ confusion.
6. _____ a new language _____ a lot of practice.

Consumer Smarts

CHALLENGE 1 ► Comparative and superlative adjectives—Part 1

	Simple	Comparative	Superlative	Rule
Short adjectives	small slow	smaller slower	smallest slowest	Add **-er** or **-est** to the end of the adjective.
Long adjectives	beautiful	more beautiful	most beautiful	Add **more** or **most** before the adjective.
Irregular adjectives	good bad	better worse	best worst	These adjectives are irregular.

- Use **than** after a comparative adjective followed by a noun: A letter is cheaper **than** a phone call.
- Use **the** before a superlative: The Internet is **the** cheapest form of communication.

A Use a comparative or superlative adjective to complete each sentence.

EXAMPLE: (good) Office Deals is the _____ **best** _____ place to buy office supplies.

1. (small) The Office Deals store is _____ *smaller* _____ than the Office Buys store.
2. (bad) The Office Buys store has the _____ *worst* _____ prices in town.
3. (fast) The clerks at Office Buys are _____ *faster* _____ than the ones at Office Deals.
4. (good) A CD-ROM is _____ *better* _____ than a floppy disk.
5. (slow) A bus is _____ *slower* _____ than a taxi.
6. (expensive) A taxi is _____ *more expensive* _____ than a bus.
7. (cheap) A mini is the _____ *cheapest* _____ car you can buy.
8. (expensive) Racing cars are the _____ *most expensive* _____ cars.

B Use the words to write comparative or superlative sentences.

EXAMPLE: this restaurant / good / that one
___*This restaurant is better than that one.*___

1. cars / fast / bicycles
   Cars are faster than bicycles.
2. airplanes / fast / way to travel
   Airplanes are the fastest way to travel.
3. sandals / comfortable / high-heeled shoes
   Sandals are more comfortable than high-heeled shoes.
4. sneakers / comfortable / kind of shoe
   Sneakers are the most comfortable kind of shoe
5. pasta / cheap / steak
   Pasta is cheaper than steak.
6. coffee / cheap / item on the menu
   Coffee is the cheapest item on the menu.

UNIT 2 Consumer Smarts

CHALLENGE 2 ► Comparative and superlative adjectives —Part 2

	Simple	Comparative	Superlative	Rule Comparative	Rule Superlative
Adjectives that end in **-e**	large	larger	largest	add **-r**	add **-st**
Adjectives that end in **-y**	pretty	prettier	prettiest	change the **y** to **i** and add **-er**	change the **y** to **i** and add **-est**
Adjectives that end in *consonant-vowel-consonant*	big	bigger	biggest	double the final consonant and add **-er**	double the final consonant and add **-est**

• Some two-syllable adjectives have two correct forms:
   quiet/quieter/quietest and **quiet/more quiet/ most quiet.**

 A Find the mistake in each sentence and correct it.

EXAMPLE: Going to a car wash is *easier* ~~easyer~~ than washing your own car.

1. Going to a car wash is also more expensiver than washing your own car.
2. I think pizza is healthy than hamburgers.
3. Pontillo's has the better pizza in town.
4. Their pizza is always more hot than Angelo's pizza.
5. Pontillo's is also more closer than Angelo's.
6. This computer is more heavy than my old one.
7. It's also quiet than my old one.
8. This computer also has a biger screen than my old one.

B Fill in the correct comparative form (adjective + *than*) or superlative form (*the* + superlative).

Terron	1-year-old car	cost $26,000	OK tires	drives carefully
Lisa	5-year-old car	cost $13,000	bad tires	drives very fast
Bob	9-year-old car	cost $32,000	great tires	doesn't drive well

EXAMPLE: (new) Lisa's car is _____ *newer than* _____ Bob's car.

1. (old)   Bob's car is _____ of all.
2. (nice)   Terron's car is probably _____ Bob's.
3. (expensive) Bob's car was _____ Lisa's.
4. (big)   Bob's car is probably _____ Lisa's.
5. (pretty)   Lisa thinks her car is _____ of all.
6. (good)   Terron's tires are _____ Lisa's.

UNIT 2 Consumer Smarts

CHALLENGE 3 ▶ Imperatives

Negative	Base form	Complement
	Shop	carefully.
Don't	buy	the cheapest item.
	Compare	prices.
Do not	spend	more than you can afford!

- Use the imperative form to give instructions or commands.
- The subject of the imperative is **you,** but don't include it in the statement.
- For negative imperatives, the full form, **Do not** is stronger than the contraction **Don't.**
- **Be** can be used in imperatives: Don't **be** late. **Be** quiet.
- Use an exclamation mark (**!**) to show strong feeling: Watch out**!**

A Your friend is buying a new car. Tell him or her what to do. Use verbs from the box.

borrow	~~buy~~	look at	read	accept	sit	drive	ask	compare

EXAMPLE: _____**Don't buy**_____ the first car you see.

1. _____ the first price the salesperson gives you.
2. _____ the car before you buy it.
3. _____ a lot of questions.
4. _____ too much money.
5. _____ a lot of different cars.
6. _____ in the seats.
7. _____ about the car in magazines.
8. _____ prices at different car dealerships.

B Complete the conversation. Use verbs from the box.

wear	wait	leave	use	keep	open	~~try~~	spray	inhale	wipe

STUDENT A: I really need to clean this floor.

STUDENT B: (1) _____**Try**_____ Clean-eze. It's really strong!

STUDENT A: How does it work?

STUDENT B: (2) _____ it on the floor. (3) _____ it for a few minutes. (4) _____ it up right away. (5) _____ five minutes. Then (6) _____ a soft cloth to polish it.

STUDENT A: Should I (7) _____ gloves?

STUDENT B: That's not necessary. But (8) _____ the windows and (9) _____ any Clean-eze. It's bad for you.

STUDENT A: Anything else I should know?

STUDENT B: (10) _____ it away from children.

STUDENT A: You know, maybe I'll try soap and water instead.

CHALLENGE 4 ▸ Transition words

Using numbers	Not using numbers
First, (First of all,)	First,
Second, (Secondly,)	Next,
Third, (Thirdly,)	Then,
	After that,
Lastly, (Finally,)	Lastly, (Finally,)

- Do not use numbers as transition words if more than four steps are being described.
- When not using numbers, the words **then** and **after that** can be used to begin several sentences.
- Finish with the word **Lastly** or **Finally.**

A Use the following sentences to write two different paragraphs. Add transition words that use numbers at the beginning of the sentences.

Make your purchases.
Decide if this is the right bank for you.
Ask your friends where they get their clothes.
Choose a bank near your home.

Talk to the bank manager.
Visit each store.
Go home and think about what she said.
Compare prices of similar items.

Paragraph 1   Title: Buying New Clothes

**First, ask your friends where they get their clothes.** _____

_____

_____

Paragraph 2   Title: Finding the Right Bank

_____

_____

_____

B Complete the sentences with transition words that don't use numbers. (More than one transition word may be correct for some sentences.)

Owning a car isn't always easy. (1) _____ _**First**_ _____, you need to find a car that isn't too expensive. (2) _____ you have to find a place to park it when you aren't using it. If you live in a city this may be difficult. (3) _____, you need to find insurance you can afford. (4) _____, you can start thinking about how to pay for gas and oil and tires and repairs. (5) _____, there is usually a wait of several weeks (or even months) before the car arrives. (6) _____ you get your car! After all that, are you sure you really want it?

CHALLENGE 5 ▶ Causative with *get*

Subject	*Get*	Object	Past participle	
I	**get**	my car	washed	every Saturday.
We	**got**	our picture	taken.	
They	**will get**	the roof	fixed	next year.

- Causative verbs show that the subject causes something to happen.
- Any tense of the verb **get** can be used.

A Unscramble the words to make causative sentences.

EXAMPLE: refrigerator / I / got / fixed / the   ___*I got the refrigerator fixed.*___

1. house / he / the / gets / cleaned / once a week   _____
2. she / watch / fixed / got / her   _____
3. she / her check / got / cashed / at the bank   _____
4. will get / their eyes / they / tested   _____
5. car / we / will get / repaired / the   _____
6. he / motor oil / changed / got / his   _____
7. get / their picture / they / taken / every year   _____
8. my hair / will / I / cut / get / tomorrow   _____

B Rewrite each sentence using a causative with *get*.

EXAMPLE: My uncle will fix my stereo tomorrow. I ___*will get my stereo fixed tomorrow.*___

1. The dry cleaner cleaned my coat.
   I _____
2. They wash my clothes at the laundromat.
   I _____
3. My brother painted the living room for me.
   I _____
4. The teacher will translate my letter.
   I _____
5. The bank corrected the mistake for me.
   I _____
6. The company will fix Terron's computer.
   Terron _____
7. My sister changed her name.
   My sister _____
8. They repair my car at the garage.
   I _____

UNIT 2 **Consumer Smarts**

CHALLENGE 6 ▶ Present tense *be* question tags

Statement	Tag question	Short answer	
That vacuum cleaner is noisy,	**isn't it?**	Yes, it is.	No, it isn't.
Those chairs are comfortable	**aren't they?**	Yes, they are.	No they aren't.
Thomas isn't in the store,	**is he?**	Yes, he is.	No, he isn't.
You aren't very comfortable	**are you?**	Yes, I am.	No, I'm not.

- The verb in the tag question is the same tense as the main verb.
- A tag question always uses a subject pronoun.

A **Choose the correct question tag. Fill in the bubble completely.**

EXAMPLE: You're Rosa, ⚪ are you? ⚫ aren't you?

1. This is your application form, ⚪ aren't you? ⚪ isn't it?
2. Your last name is Mendez, ⚪ isn't it? ⚪ is it?
3. You're from Colombia, ⚪ are you? ⚪ aren't you?
4. We're from the same country, ⚪ are we? ⚪ aren't we?
5. Your phone number is 343-1758, ⚪ is it? ⚪ isn't it?
6. Your parents aren't still in Colombia, ⚪ are they? ⚪ aren't they?
7. Your sister is a doctor, ⚪ isn't it? ⚪ isn't she?
8. You're a teacher, ⚪ are you? ⚪ aren't you?
9. Your classes aren't large, ⚪ are they? ⚪ aren't they?
10. Your husband is a banker, ⚪ isn't it? ⚪ isn't he?

B **Complete the conversation using tag questions and short answers.**

Janie: Wow! These computers are really expensive, (1) _____ ***aren't they*** _____?

Nicolai: (2) _____.

Janie: And they aren't any better than my old computer, (3) _____?

Nicolai: (4) _____.

Janie: You aren't happy with the prices either, (5) _____?

Nicolai: (6) _____.

Janie: Let's go to another store.

[later…]

Nicolai: Well, this store is a lot better, (7) _____?

Janie: (8) _____.

Nicolai: Oh, look! Here's a really cheap computer. That's a great price, (9) _____?

Janie: (10) _____.

Nicolai: You're a very careful shopper, (11) _____?

Janie: (12) _____.

UNIT
2　　**Consumer Smarts**

CHALLENGE 7 ▶ Present tense *Which* questions

QUESTIONS				ANSWERS	
Which	Subject	*Be*	Complement	Subject	*Be*
Which	diskette	is	yours?	The black one	(is).
Which	computers	are	on sale?	The Vintel computers	(are).
Which	monitor	was	cheaper?	The P543 monitor	(was).
Which	CD-ROMs	were	on sale?	The old ones	(were).

- Use **which** when there is a choice between two or more items.
- The words **one** or **ones** can be used to avoid repeating the noun in the question.
- The verb **be** can be dropped in the answer.

A　Match each question with the correct answer.

1. _*d*_ Which clothing store is your favorite?
2. ___ Which things are cheaper there?
3. ___ Which pants are on sale?
4. ___ Which jacket is really expensive?
5. ___ Which mall is open late on Saturdays?
6. ___ Which stores are the nicest?
7. ___ Which day is best for shopping?
8. ___ Which shoes are the most comfortable?

a. The red one is.
b. The newest stores are.
c. Shoes and socks.
d. The big one at the mall.
e. Thursday is.
f. My old ones.
g. The black ones are.
h. The new one on Route 56.

B　Write questions with *Which*. Use the word *one* or *ones* and the verb *be* in the answers.

EXAMPLE:　Q: (cheap / watch) _**Which watch is cheap?**_　　A: (small) _**The small one is.**_

1. Q: (the biggest / shoes) _____　A: (black) _____
2. Q: (good / tailor) _____　A: (French) _____
3. Q: (warmest / boots) _____　A: (white) _____
4. Q: (fast / bike) _____　A: (red) _____
5. Q: (the best / bikes) _____　A: (new) _____
6. Q: (the cheapest / bike) _____　A: (green) _____
7. Q: (the fastest / cars) _____　A: (Italian) _____
8. Q: (slow / car) _____　A: (old) _____
9. Q: (friendly / doctors) _____　A: (young) _____
10. Q: (cold / office) _____　A: (big) _____

CHALLENGE 8 ▶ Adjective clauses

Main clause	Adjective clause with a pronoun used as the subject		
	who, that, which	Verb	Complement
I talked to the woman	**who (that)**	works	in the store.
She sells some cleaning products	**that (which)**	are	dangerous.

Main clause	Adjective clause with a pronoun used as the object		
	whom, that, which	Subject	Verb
I talked to a woman	**whom (that)**	I	met at the store.
She sells some cleaning products	**that (which)**	we	won't buy.

- **Who** and **whom** are used for people; **which** is used for things; **that** is used for both people and things.
- **Whom, that,** and **which** can be omitted when they are the object of an adjective clause.
  She sells some cleaning products I won't buy.

A Complete each sentence with *who, whom, that,* or *which.* (Some items may have two correct answers.)

EXAMPLE: Planting flowers is something ___*that (which)*___ I like to do.

1. I like talking to people _____ know about flowers.
2. There are a lot of people _____ have gardens.
3. Some of the people _____ I meet are really interesting.
4. I just met a woman _____ works in her garden eight hours a day.
5. Gardening is a hobby _____ can take a lot of time.
6. It's something _____ I really love.

B Use adjective clauses to combine these two sentences.

EXAMPLE: The post office is on First Street. I use the post office.
       ___*The post office that I use is on First Street.*___

1. The pharmacy is on the corner. It sells inexpensive medicines.
   _____

2. The jewelry store is owned by a woman. She loves old necklaces and rings.
   _____

3. The delivery person is late. I am waiting for him.
   _____

4. The computer store is closed today. It sells mousepads.
   _____

5. The grocery store is owned by my friend. My friend sells only the freshest fruit.
   _____

6. The stereo speakers are expensive. I want them.
   _____

UNIT 3 **Housing**

CHALLENGE 1 ▶ Past continuous

STATEMENT			
Subject	***Be* (past)**	***-ing* form**	**Complement**
I	**was**	**walking**	home.
We	**were**	**talking**	with the landlord.

YES/NO QUESTION			
***Be* (past)**	**Subject**	***-ing* form**	**Complement**
Was	she	**reading**	the classified ads?
Were	they	**making**	dinner?

• The past continuous describes what was in progress at a specific moment in the past.
• Use the past continuous to describe a past scene.
   Maryanne **was talking** with the landlord. She **was standing** by the window and **pointing** at the air conditioner.

A Unscramble the words to make past continuous statements and questions.

EXAMPLE: sleeping/ was / she / .   ___*She was sleeping.*_____

1. Bo / taking / shower / a / was / .   _____
2. eating / he / was / breakfast / ?   _____
3. room / the / was / Vu / painting / ?   _____
4. were / children / the / dinner / eating / .   _____
5. I / talking / on / was / the / phone / ?   _____
6. studying / were / we / .   _____
7. making / were / they / breakfast / ?   _____
8. I / painting / hanging / was / a / .   _____

B Complete the descriptions. Use the past continuous form of the verbs in the box.

walk   eat   pay   ~~sit~~   sleep   add   ride   talk   laugh   look   write

1. Last night Maryanne and Vu _____***were sitting***_____ in the living room. They _____ some bills. They _____ also _____ about their finances. Maryanne _____ down all their expenses. Vu _____ up the numbers. The children _____ in their rooms.

2. I saw the Nguyens in the park yesterday. Vu and Maryanne _____ very slowly. They _____ at all the trees and flowers. Truyen _____ his bicycle. Bao _____ an ice cream cone. The girls _____ about something. They all looked very happy.

Housing

CHALLENGE 2 ▶ Time clauses with *when* and *while*

Time word	Shorter action	Time word	Longer action	Time word	Shorter action
	The phone rang	**while**	I was studying.		
		While	I was studying,		the phone rang.
			I was studying	**when**	the phone rang.
When	the phone rang,		I was studying.		

- Use **while** + the past continuous with a long continuing action.
- Use **when** + the simple past with a short non-continuing action.
- If the time clause precedes the main clause, use a comma.

A Circle the correct time word in each sentence.

EXAMPLE: Mrs. Jones was living in Chicago ((when) / while) she had a baby.

1. We bought a condo (when / while) we were living in a rental apartment.
2. The apartment was small so we were happy (when / while) we moved out.
3. (When / While) he was cleaning the apartment, Jim found $50.
4. He was really excited (when / while) he showed it to me.
5. We were talking about how to spend it (when / while) the phone rang.
6. The children stayed with my parents (when / while) we were packing our things.
7. (When / While) they were staying there, they visited the zoo.
8. They were still talking about the zoo trip (when / while) they got home a week later.

B Combine the sentences.

EXAMPLE: It started to rain. We were standing on the balcony.
           While *we were standing on the balcony, it started to rain.*

1. I was talking with the security guard. She got a phone call.
    While _____

2. The rain stopped. We were looking out the window.
    _____ when _____

3. I was doing the laundry. The dryer broke.
    While _____

4. I saw you. You were leaving the house.
    When _____

5. I was cleaning the living room. I turned on the air conditioning.
    _____ while _____

6. I closed the garage door. I was washing the car.
    While _____

7. We stopped for a snack. We were shopping for furniture.
    _____ while _____

UNIT 3 Housing

CHALLENGE 3 ▶ Present tense *yes/no* questions and answers with *ever*

Do/Does	Subject	*Ever*	Base form	Complement	Short answer
Do	you	**ever**	swim	in the pool?	Yes, we **often** do. No, we **never** do.
Does	she	**ever**	wash	the windows?	Yes, she **sometimes** does. No, she **never** does.
Do	they	**ever**	use	the dryer?	Yes, they **frequently** do. No, they **never** do.

- Use **ever** in *yes/no* questions when an answer that has a frequency word is wanted.
- In the short answer, the frequency word comes after the subject and before the verb.
- **Always, usually, often, sometimes, seldom**, and **rarely** are used with affirmative verbs.
- When **never** is used in a short answer, the verb is affirmative.

A Use the words to write *yes/no* questions with *ever*.

EXAMPLE: Pablo / make dinner   *Does Pablo ever make dinner?*

1. Pablo / clean the refrigerator   _____
2. Mr. Mendez / see the landlord   _____
3. Rachel / read the newspaper   _____
4. Mr. Mendez / forget to pay a bill   _____
5. Pablo / make breakfast   _____
6. Rachel / use the washer and dryer   _____
7. Pablo / take out the trash   _____
8. Mr. Mendez / make dinner   _____
9. Rachel / clean her room   _____
10. Mr. Mendez / walk the dog   _____

B Match the questions with the answers.

EXAMPLE: __*a*__ Does Victor go swimming on the weekend?   a̶. No, he seldom does.

1. _____ Does Rachel read the newspaper every morning?   b. Yes, you often do.
2. _____ Do you always read the classified ads on Sunday?   c. Yes, she always does.
3. _____ Do we always pay their bills on time?   d. Yes, it frequently does.
4. _____ Do the Masons often complain about the rent?   e. No, they rarely do.
5. _____ Do I ever ask you to clean the house?   f. Yes, I usually do.
6. _____ Does the refrigerator often make that noise?   g. Yes, we always do.

CHALLENGE 4 ▶ Comparison with *more/fewer/less* and *most/fewest/least*

Example	Explanation
This building has **more** balconies than that one. That building has **fewer** balconies than this one.	Use **more** or **fewer** to compare count nouns.
Our new house uses **more** heat than our old one. Our old house used **less** heat than our new one.	Use **more** or **less** to compare non-count nouns.
Apartment A has **the most** windows. Apartment F has **the fewest** windows.	Use **the most** or **the fewest** for count nouns.
Apartment C has **the most** space. Apartment F has **the least** space.	Use **the most** or **the least** for non-count nouns.

A Use one of the expressions in the box to complete each sentence.

more	fewer	less	the most	the fewest	the least

EXAMPLE: Nguyen's room is the biggest. It has _____ ***the most*** _____ space.

1. The Rivera family pays $1000 rent and the Nguyens pay $750.
    The Nguyens pay _____ rent than the Riveras.

2. Mr. Nguyen has two credit cards and Mrs. Truong has three.
    Mrs. Truong has _____ credit cards than Mr. Nguyen.

3. The Nguyens have four children, Mr. Rivera has two, and Mrs. Nassab has one.
    Mrs. Nassab has _____ children.
    Mr. Rivera has _____ children than the Nguyens.

4. Vu's apartment is very sunny, but Mrs. Nassab's apartment isn't.
    Mrs. Nassab's apartment gets _____ sun than Vu's.

5. Vu's apartment has two bedrooms but Mrs. Nassab's has three.
    Vu's apartment has _____ bedrooms than Mrs. Nassab's.

6. Mrs. Nassab's building has 14 children, Mr. Rivera's building has 10, and Vu's building has 7.
    Vu's building has _____ children.
    Mrs. Nassab's building has _____ children.

B Correct the error in each sentence.

EXAMPLE: We have ~~most~~ *more* problems with our landlord than you do.

1. We have the few apartments in our building than you do.

2. My sister has most children than any of her friends

3. I have fewest children than my sister.

4. I pay the less rent of anyone in my family.

5. My father pays the more rent of all.

CHALLENGE 5 ► Short answers to questions containing *when* and *while* clauses

Question with *when* and *while* clauses	Short answer
Was Truyen talking with the landlord **when** you saw him?	Yes, he **was.**
Did he notice you **while** he was talking?	No, he **didn't.**
When you saw them, **were** they standing on the balcony?	Yes, they **were.**
While you were watching them, **did** they go inside?	No, they **didn't.**

- For short answers, use the verb tense of the main clause, not the verb tense of the time clause.
- Use **was/wasn't** and **were/weren't** for past continuous short answers.
- Use **did/didn't** for simple past short answers.

A Match each question with the correct answer.

EXAMPLE: ___*f*___ Were they cleaning the apartment when the new furniture arrived?

1. _____ While you were waiting, did you read the rental agreement?
2. _____ Did Vu take notes while he was inspecting the condo?
3. _____ While they were talking, did they open the windows?
4. _____ Was I at work while you were looking at apartments?
5. _____ Were you surprised when you saw the apartment?
6. _____ Did they get a phone call while you were looking around?
7. _____ When the landlord arrived, was he carrying a briefcase?
8. _____ Did you sit down while you were talking to the landlord?

a. Yes, you were.
b. No, they didn't.
c. Yes, he was.
d. Yes, I did.
e. No, he didn't.
f. Yes, they were.
g. No, I didn't.
h. No, I wasn't.
i. Yes, they did.

B Complete the short answers.

EXAMPLE: While Vu was paying the bill, did he check the addition? Yes, ___*he did.*___

1. Did he ask questions while he was talking to the representative? Yes, _____
2. While they were talking, did he ask the price? Yes, _____
3. Was he smiling when he heard the price? No, _____
4. Did you ask the price while you were talking to him? No, _____
5. Were the Truongs waiting when the landlord arrived? Yes, _____
6. Did the landlord mention the agreement while they were talking? No, _____
7. When they left, were the Truongs smiling? Yes, _____
8. While they were walking down the street, did they start laughing? No, _____
9. Was Vu eating dinner when the landlord called back? Yes, _____
10. Did he continue to eat while he was talking on the phone? No, _____

CHALLENGE 6 ► *Very, too,* and *enough* with adjectives and adverbs

Statements with *very, too,* and *enough*	Meaning
This house is **very small.**	It's not big; it's tiny.
It's **too small** for my family.	We can't live there. We need more space.
It's **big enough** for one person.	One person can live there comfortably.
The landlord speaks **very fast.**	She doesn't speak slowly.
She speaks **too fast.**	I can't understand her.
She doesn't speak **slowly enough.**	I need her to speak more slowly.

- **Very** is a neutral word. Put **very** before an adjective or adverb.
- **Too** indicates that there is a problem. Put **too** before an adjective or adverb.
- **Enough** means "as much or as many as needed." Put **enough** after an adjective or adverb.

A **Write *very, too,* or *enough* in each blank.**

EXAMPLE: This house has a _____ **very** _____ big back yard.

1.   A studio apartment is _____ small for a family.

2.   I like this house. It's _____ big.

3.   It's big _____ for a large family.

4.   The garage is great. It's _____ wide.

5.   It's wide _____ for both of our cars.

6.   And the neighbors are _____ friendly.

7.   But the price is _____ high. We can't afford it.

8.   Few houses have prices that are low _____.

9.   I hope it's not _____ late for us.

10.   I hope we can find the right house _____ soon.

B **Complete the sentences using *very, too,* or *enough* and the word in parentheses.**

EXAMPLE: The family couldn't rent the apartment. (expensive)   It was **too expensive** _____.

1.   They liked the carpeting. (beautiful)   It was _____.

2.   The dining room was OK for four people. (big)   It was _____.

3.   The appliances were also OK. (new)   They were _____.

4.   There was one bedroom for four people. (small)   The apartment was _____.

5.   The rent was so high they couldn't afford it. (high)   The rent was _____.

6.   The landlord was friendly and helpful. (nice)   He was _____.

7.   The neighborhood wasn't safe. (dangerous)   It was _____.

8.   The schools were too far away. (near)   They weren't _____.

UNIT
3   **Housing**

CHALLENGE 7 ▶ *Should, must,* and *have to*

Statement with modal	Explanation
You **should** sign a rental agreement.	Use **should** to give advice.
You **shouldn't** sign a blank agreement.	Use **shouldn't** to give advice.
The agreement **must** list the rent.	**Must** shows necessity.
The landlord **must not** ask your nationality.	**Must not** shows that something is against the rules.
The tenant **has to** sign the lease.	**Has to** shows necessity.
Other family members **don't have to** sign it.	**Don't/Doesn't have to** shows that something isn't necessary.

- **Have to** is more common than **must** for personal necessity.
- **Must** is stronger and usually tells about laws or rules.

A   Circle the correct word or words to complete each sentence.

EXAMPLE: The tenant ((must) / should) sign the lease.

1.   The tenant (has to / should) read the rental agreement very carefully.
2.   The tenants (have to / should) supply their own furniture.
3.   The landlord (must / should) fix the appliances.
4.   The landlord (has to / should) keep the building clean.
5.   Most tenants (have to / should) pay a security deposit.
6.   The tenants (don't have to / shouldn't) make too much noise.
7.   The landlord (doesn't have to / must not) visit the building every day.
8.   The tenant (doesn't have to / should) keep a copy of the rental agreement.
9.   The tenants (don't have to / must) pay the rent every month.
10.   If there is a problem, the tenant (must not / should) speak to the landlord in person.

B   Fill in the circle to complete each sentence correctly.

EXAMPLE: All families ___ have a budget.   ○ have to   ● should   ○ shouldn't

1.   Your expenses ___ be more than your income.   ○ have to   ○ should   ○ shouldn't
2.   People ___ have cable TV. It's not really necessary.   ○ must   ○ should   ○ don't have to
3.   If you get cable TV, you ___ pay for it each month.   ○ shouldn't   ○ must   ○ should
4.   To increase family income, some kids ___ get jobs.   ○ shouldn't   ○ have to   ○ don't have to
5.   When you move, you ___ cancel the utilities.   ○ have to   ○ should   ○ don't have to
6.   You ___ read your utility bills carefully.   ○ have to   ○ should   ○ shouldn't
7.   You ___ learn how to write a business letter.   ○ must   ○ should   ○ have to
8.   Most children ___ pay rent to their parents.   ○ should   ○ must   ○ don't have to

UNIT 3 Housing

CHALLENGE 8 ▸ Questions with *How much*

PRESENT AND PAST—*BE*		
How much	**Be**	**Subject**
How much	is	that refrigerator?
How much	was	the deposit?

• Use **how much** + **be** to ask about prices.

PRESENT AND PAST—OTHER VERBS				
How much	**Non-count noun**	**Helping verb**	**Subject**	**Base form**
How much	money	do	we	have?
How much	furniture	does	she	need?
How much	cash	did	you	take?
How much	information	did	the landlord	supply?

• Use **how much** with non-count nouns to ask about quantities.

A Use the words and phrases in the box to complete the conversation.

> did we use   did you pay   was   did we pay   do we have   did you earn   do we need   is

May: How much money (1) ___***do we have***___ ?
Vu: About $500. How much
         (2) _____ the electric bill?
May: It's $140. How much electricity
         (3) _____?
Vu: A lot, I guess! Good thing I got a raise.
May: How much (4) _____ your raise?
Vu: It was $150 a month. Now, how much
         (5) _____ for groceries last month?

May: Almost $900.
Vu: Whew! How much food (6) _____
         for this family?
May: We eat a lot.
Vu: How much (7) _____ this
         month?
May: Over a thousand dollars.
Vu: And how much tax (8) _____?
May: Don't ask!

B Use the words to write questions with *How much.*

EXAMPLE: information / your sister / get (past)   ___*How much information did your sister get?*___

1. traffic / you /see (past)   _____
2. space / you / need (present)   _____
3. light / the apartment / have (present)   _____
4. be / your rent (present)   _____
5. furniture / they / leave behind (past)   _____
6. food / you / buy (past)   _____
7. time / the move / take (past)   _____
8. be / the bill (past)   _____

UNIT 4   Our Community

CHALLENGE 1 ▶ *Wh-* questions with *be*

Wh- word	*Be*	Subject
Who	**are**	those people?
What	**is**	your name?
When	**was**	the children's story hour?
Where	**were**	the librarians yesterday?

• In conversation, contractions can be made with **wh-** words + **be**: **Who's** that? **What're** these? **Where's** your father?
• Questions with **what** sometimes ask for a definition.
   What is a library fine? It's money you pay when you lose a book.

A Complete each library question with a word from each box.

who	what	when	where

is	are	was	were

EXAMPLE: Q: _____**Where**_____ _____**are**_____ the hardcover books?   A: They're over there.

1. Q: _____ _____ an overdue book?   A: It's a book that someone forgot to bring back.
2. Q: _____ _____ the videos?   A: They were downstairs.
3. Q: _____ _____ that woman?   A: She's the librarian.
4. Q: _____ _____ the library open?   A: It was open from 9:00 A.M. to 5:00 P.M.
5. Q: _____ _____ a replacement card?   A: You get one when you lose your library card.
6. Q: _____ _____ my library card?   A: It's in your pocket.
7. Q: _____ _____ those men?   A: They're my classmates.
8. Q: _____ _____ those books?   A: They were reference books.

B Read the answers. Write *wh-* questions with *be*.

EXAMPLE: Q: _____*What's that?*_____   A: It's my driver's license.

1. Q: _____   A: That's a DMV clerk.
2. Q: _____   A: The DMV was about a mile from here.
3. Q: _____   A: It's open at 7:30.
4. Q: _____   A: A directory is a list of people's names.
5. Q: _____   A: That was my older sister.
6. Q: _____   A: My new registration form was on the table.
7. Q: _____   A: That's my old registration form.
8. Q: _____   A: My test is in ten minutes.
9. Q: _____   A: A clerk is a person working in an office.
10. Q: _____   A: The information desk is over there.

CHALLENGE 2 ▶ *How far, How often, What time*

Phrase	*do/does/did*	Subject	Base form	Complement	Answer
How far	do	you	walk	to work?	About three miles.
How often	did	they	take	a bus?	Once a week.
What time	does	she	leave	the house?	At 8:30.

- Other **How often** answers include: **every day, once a month,** and **from time to time.**
- Other **What time** answers include: **in the morning, in the afternoon, in the evening,** and **at night.**

A   **Correct the error in each question.**

EXAMPLE: Q: ~~How often~~ *How far* did the bus take you?   A: Six miles.

1. Q: What time did you put money in your account?   A: Every week.

2. Q: How far is the bank manager there?   A: Every day but Sunday.

3. Q: How often does the bank open?   A: At 9:00 in the morning.

4. Q: What time does she check her balance?   A: Once a week.

5. Q: What time do you live from the bank?   A: Three blocks.

6. Q: How often does the bank close?   A: At 3:00 in the afternoon.

7. Q: How often is the bank from your office?   A: It's just around the corner.

8. Q: How far do the tellers leave work?   A: At 4:00.

B   **Complete the questions in this conversation. Use *How far, How often,* or *What time.***

Bob: Hey, Marcia. (1) ____**How often**____ do you go to the bank?

Marcia: I go every Friday. (2) _____ do you go?

Bob: I never go. I do my banking by computer.

Marcia: Does it really save time?

Bob: Just think. (3) _____ do you go to the bank?

Marcia: At about 3:00 in the afternoon.

Bob: And (4) _____ is it to the bank?

Marcia: It's about fifteen minutes away.

Bob: And (5) _____ do you have to wait for a teller?

Marcia: Always!

Bob: See?

Marcia: Well, (6) _____ do you do your banking?

Bob: I usually do it at 10:00 at night.

Marcia: And (7) _____ do you check your account?

Bob: At least once a week.

Marcia: And (8) _____ are the bank's computers closed down?

Bob: Never.

Marcia: Wow! (9) _____ does the bank open tomorrow?

Bob: At 9:00. But you can open an account from your home computer.

Marcia: Great! And (10) _____ can I check my balance?

Bob: Every ten minutes, if you want.

UNIT 4 ▶ Our Community

CHALLENGE 3 ▶ Past tense time clauses

Main clause	Time clause
I got my driver's license	**before** I registered my car.
I registered my car	**after** I finished work on Friday.
I was really excited	**when** I passed my driver's test.

- The time clause can go before or after the main clause.
- Use a comma after the time clause when it comes at the beginning of the sentence.

    After I got my driver's license, I registered my car.

- **When** means "at that time" or "shortly after that time."

A Match each main clause with the correct time clause.

EXAMPLE: I made an appointment for the road test _**e**_ .

1. I left home early and the DMV opened just ___.
2. There were not a lot of people in line ___.
3. I was really nervous ___.
4. I felt much better ___.
5. I picked up my license ___.
6. I gave all my friends rides to school ___.
7. I walked everywhere ___.
8. I asked my friends to pay for gas ___.

a. before I left the DMV that day
b. after I got my license
c. before I took my test
d. after I arrived
e. after I practiced driving for several weeks
f. when I didn't have any money
g. when I got there
h. before I bought my own car
i. after I finished the test

B Write past tense sentences with time clauses. Use commas when necessary.

EXAMPLE: after / Eric and Susan / move to Florida / be very happy
   After Eric and Susan moved to Florida, they were very happy.

1. before / they / leave / New York / never exercise

   _____

2. Susan / join / health club / when / arrive in Florida

   _____

3. after / Susan join / the health club / Eric join, too

   _____

4. they / join the club / before / find a house to live in

   _____

5. they / be very happy / when / find the right house

   _____

6. before / they / move in / paint all the rooms

   _____

7. when / they / finish all their work / house / looked great

   _____

Time clauses with future meaning

CHALLENGE 4 ▶ Time clauses with future meaning

Main clause	Time clause
I'll review for the test	**before** I go to class tomorrow.
Gloria will take a shower	**after** she gets home.
My children will take piano lessons	**when** they are ready.
They won't practice	**until** I tell them to.

• Use the future tense in the main clause and the simple present in the time clause.
• **Until** means "up to that time."

A Use the verbs in the box to complete the sentences.

find   go   finish   ~~have~~   visit   get   help   stay   write

EXAMPLE: I'll get a library card when I _____**have**_____ the time.

1. My children _____ to the library when the teacher asks them to.

2. I will talk to them before they _____ the library.

3. When they ask the librarian questions, she _____ them find the answers.

4. They will look for the answers until they _____ them.

5. After they find the answers, they _____ them down.

6. They _____ at the library until they finish all their work.

7. After they _____, I will take them for ice cream.

8. They will want to watch TV when they _____ home.

B Use the words *before, after, when,* and *until* to complete the paragraphs.

Mario will register for an adult education class (1) _____**after**_____ he finishes work today. He will pay a small fee (2) _____ he registers for the class. He will buy the textbook (3) _____ the first class so that he is sure to get one. But he won't read the book (4) _____ the teacher gives an assignment.

(5) _____ he goes to the first class, he will see a lot of new people. He won't talk to anyone (6) _____ someone talks to him. He will meet someone nice (7) _____ he leaves the class. They will go out for coffee (8) _____ they leave the class.

(9) _____ he leaves the class, Mario will say goodbye to the teacher. (10) _____ he does this, the teacher will smile and shake his hand. (11) _____ he says goodbye, Mario and his new friend will leave. They will sit and drink coffee (12) _____ it is time to go home.

CHALLENGE 5 ▶ Prepositions of location

Preposition	Use	Example
in	Before a city, state, or country name	Rochelle lives **in** San Francisco.
on	Before a street name	Bob lives **on** Fifth Avenue.
at	Before a street address, street intersection, or building name	I live **at** 79 Main Street. The school is **at** State and Main.
next to	Describes two objects beside each other	The school is **next to** the post office on State Street.
across from	Describes two objects facing each other on opposite sides of an open area	The hotel is **across from** the post office on State Street.

A **Complete the conversation. Use *in, on, at, next to,* and *across from*.**

Carlos: Is there an art museum (1) _____**in**_____ Centerville?

Steve: Sure. It's (2) _____ Elm Street.

Carlos: Is it (3) _____ the high school?

Steve: No, it's across the street from the high school. It's (4) _____ 450 Elm Street.

Carlos: Oh, I know. And is there a bus stop (5) _____ the art museum?

Steve: No, but there's one (6) _____ the corner of Elm Street and Center Street.

Carlos: I visited a great museum when I was (7) _____ England.

Steve: Is the museum (8) _____ London?

Carlos: Yes. It's called the Little Museum.

Steve: Is it next to the park (9) _____ Lester Street?

Carlos: No, it's (10) _____ the park.

Steve: Oh, that's right.

B **Read the sentences. Number the places on the map.**

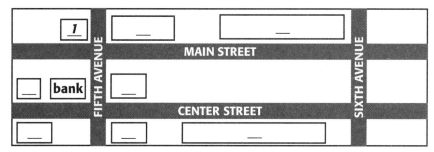

1. There is a subway stop at the corner of Fifth Avenue and Main Street.
2. There is a Japanese restaurant across from the subway stop.
3. There is a hotel next to the Japanese restaurant
4. There is a grocery store next to the bank.
5. There is an Italian restaurant across from the grocery store.
6. There is a furniture store across from the bank.
7. There is a pharmacy at the corner of Fifth Avenue and Center Street.
8. There is a department store on Center Street.

Irregular past tense verbs

CHALLENGE 6 ▶ Irregular simple past tense verbs

Irregular verb type	Base form and simple past tense	Example
No change from base form	cost/cost, put/put	This book cost $5 last year. I put the baby to bed last night.
Verbs ending in -d with t past forms	send/sent, spend/spent	I sent two letters to my family this week.
Verbs with vowel changes	leave/left, lose/lost, wake/woke, get/got, come/came, buy/bought, tell/told, read/read*	They left for Mexico yesterday.
Other changes	be/was and were, do/did, go/went, have/had, make/made	

• The simple past tense **read** is pronounced like the color **red**.

A Circle the correct verb forms.

Last week I (1) (lose / (lost)) my driver's license. It (2) (is / was) a real surprise because I don't usually (3) (do / did) things like that. My friends (4) (are / were) as surprised as I (5) (am / was). I almost never (6) (lose /lost) things. When students (7) (lose / lost) things, we usually (8) (make / made) signs and the teacher (9) (put / puts) them up on the wall. When I took the paper for the sign out of my locker, I (10) (find / found) my license. It (11) (is / was) on the floor. I (12) (tell / told) my friends and they all laughed.

B Fill in each blank with the simple past tense of the verb in parentheses.

EXAMPLE: (be) I _____**was**_____ really busy yesterday.

1. The night before, I (go) _____ to the movies with my friends.
2. Afterwards, we (spend) _____ a couple of hours watching TV at Jim's house.
3. I (leave) _____ at midnight and (get) _____ home around 1:00 A.M.
4. I (wake) _____ up at 8:00 the next morning.
5. I (put) _____ on my clothes and (have) _____ breakfast.
6. Then I (buy) _____ the newspaper and (read) _____ it.
7. My father (come) _____ home around 9:00.
8. He (send) _____ me to the grocery store to buy food.
9. The rest of the day I (do) _____ chores around the house.
10. Finally, I (leave) _____ so I wouldn't have to do anything else.

UNIT 4 — Our Community

CHALLENGE 7 ▶ *Borrow, lend,* and *owe*

Subject	Verb	Indirect object	Direct object
My brother	**will lend**	me	five dollars.
I	**will owe**	him	five dollars.

- **Lend** means "let someone use something for a period of time."
- **Owe** means "have to give back or pay back."

Subject	Verb	Direct object	*From*	Indirect object
I	**will borrow**	five dollars	from	my brother.

- **Borrow** means "use something for a period of time."
- **Borrow** is followed by direct object + **from** + indirect object. You can't say: I will **borrow** my brother five dollars.

A ▶ Match the sentences that mean the same thing.

EXAMPLE: __g__ Would you lend me some money?

1. _____ I borrowed some money from Kim Su.
2. _____ Please pay back the $5.00 you borrowed.
3. _____ I'll lend you $5.00.
4. _____ She can use my car this weekend.
5. _____ Don't let Gloria borrow any money from you.
6. _____ Can I borrow $5.00?
7. _____ I let her use my car yesterday.
8. _____ She has to pay me $5.00 for the gas she used.

a. Don't lend her money.
b. Can you lend me $5.00?
c. She owes me $5.00.
d. You can borrow $5.00.
e. I'll lend her my car.
f. You owe me $5.00.
g. Can I borrow some money?
h. She borrowed my car.
i. She lent me the money.

B ▶ Use the correct form of the verbs *borrow, lend,* and *owe* to complete each paragraph.

Jeeva wants to register his car, but he doesn't have enough money. He plans to (1) __borrow__ some money from Rochelle. He hopes she will (2) _____ him at least $25. He would like to (3) _____ twice that much, but he doesn't want to (4) _____ her $50.

Kim Su decided to (5) _____ some money from her brother. Now she (6) _____ him $30. He wanted to (7) _____ her $10, but she needed to (8) _____ more.

Carlos lost a book that he (9) _____ from the library. Now he (10) _____ the library $19.95 and he can't (11) _____ any more books until he pays the fee. He hopes Steve will (12) _____ him the money to pay for the book.

UNIT 4 Our Community

Verb + infinitive, verb + object + infinitive

CHALLENGE 8 ▸ Verb + infinitive, verb + object + infinitive

Subject	Verb	Infinitive phrase
I	**want**	**to cash** a check.
Mario	**needs**	**to open** a bank account.
They	**like**	**to use** the ATM.

Subject	Verb	Object	Infinitive phrase
I	**want**	**you**	**to lend** me $10.00.
Gloria	**needs**	**Jim**	**to sign** this check.
We	**asked**	**Mario**	**to write** a new check.

- Infinitives commonly follow these verbs: **ask, agree, begin, continue, decide, expect, forget, hope, learn, like, need, plan, try,** and **want.**
- The object + infinitive form commonly follows only these verbs from the list above: **ask, expect, like, need,** and **want.**

A Unscramble the words to make correct sentences.

EXAMPLE: want / they / me / sign / some papers / to ___*They want me to sign some papers.*___

1. need / they / write / a check / me / to _____
2. see / plan / I / them / this afternoon / to _____
3. expect / arrive / them / I / at 1:00 / to _____
4. see / hope / them sooner / I / to _____
5. wait / expect / they / me / for them / to _____
6. need / do some shopping / I / to _____
7. will / finish early / try / I / to _____
8. won't / meet them / I / forget / to _____

B Complete each sentence using a verb from each box.

ask	begin	try	~~learn~~	expect	agree	decide	want	plan
open	eat	give	let	~~use~~	have	arrive	sit	leave

EXAMPLE: I ___*learned*___ ___*to use*___ the ATM yesterday.

1. I _____ _____ a savings account in a week or two.
2. The teller _____ _____ me 200 checks when I asked a second time.
3. The customers _____ _____ at 9:00 this morning.
4. The teller _____ the bank _____ a busy day.
5. She was tired, so she _____ _____ down.
6. She _____ _____ lunch at noon, but she couldn't.
7. She _____ _____, but the boss wouldn't let her go.
8. She _____ him _____ her go, but he said no.

CHALLENGE 1 ▶ Present perfect—Part 1

	STATEMENT				QUESTION		
Subject	*Have*	Past participle		*Have*	Subject	Past participle	
I	**have**	**finished**	my work.	**Have**	you	**finished**	your work?
Darla	**has**	**had**	a cold.	**Has**	she	**had**	a cold?
They	**have**	**visited**	Maria.	**Have**	they	**visited**	Maria?

- The present perfect describes situations that started in the past and continue into the present.
- The present perfect uses a form of the verb **have** + a past participle.
- Some verbs have the same past tense form and past participle form.

A Study the list below. Write *S* for verbs with the same past tense and past participle. Write *D* for verbs with different forms.

EXAMPLE: __*D*__ grow grew grown

		Base form	Past tense	Past participle			Base form	Past tense	Past participle
1.	___	work	worked	worked	6.	___	wait	waited	waited
2.	___	see	saw	seen	7.	___	leave	left	left
3.	___	have	had	had	8.	___	take	took	taken
4.	___	visit	visited	visited	9.	___	know	knew	known
5.	___	be	was/were	been	10.	___	eat	ate	eaten

B Complete each sentence with the correct past participle from exercise A.

EXAMPLE: How many pills have you _____**taken**_____ ?

1. Has Ali _____ the doctor yet?

2. Dr. Smith has _____ at this hospital for ten years.

3. She's an old friend. I have _____ her for fifteen years.

4. We have _____ sick all week.

5. Has Gloria _____ long for the doctor to arrive?

6. Peter has _____ a cold since December.

7. Have you _____ your sister in the hospital?

8. Has she _____ any food today?

9. I'm sorry, but the doctor has _____ the hospital.

10. You have _____ three inches this year!

CHALLENGE 2 ▶ Present perfect—Part 2

Example	Explanation
He **has worked** here for ten years.	An action that continues from the past to the present
I **have seen** the doctor twice this month.	A repeated past action that is completed
They **have lived** in France.	A past action that does not mention a specific time

- The present perfect has three different meanings.
- The contractions **'s** and **'ve** can be used in affirmative statements.
    He**'s** worked here for ten years. They**'ve** lived in France.
- The contractions **hasn't** and **haven't** can be used in negative statements.
    I **haven't** talked with Dr. Perkins. He **hasn't** examined me.

A Write *a, b,* or *c* in the blank to show the meaning of the present perfect in each sentence.

    a. past action continuing up to present

    b. repeated past action

    c. past action without specific time

EXAMPLE: **_a_**   Have you had this backache for a long time?

1. _____ He's studied dentistry.
2. _____ She's been sick since August.
3. _____ How many colds have you had this year?
4. _____ Has the doctor ever worked in China?
5. _____ How many times have you checked your blood pressure today?
6. _____ My grandmother has had more than one stroke.
7. _____ I have had a cavity once before.
8. _____ Have you gained weight since you stopped smoking?

B Use the words to make sentences with the present perfect. Use contractions.

EXAMPLE: I / not feel / well all week   _I haven't felt well all week._ _____

1. she / not visit / me   _____
2. he / take / all the medicine   _____
3. they / not be / well   _____
4. she / have / three colds   _____
5. you / wait / more than an hour   _____
6. we / see / another doctor   _____
7. I / gain / five pounds / this week   _____
8. he / not work / there in the past   _____

CHALLENGE 3 ▶ *For* and *since*

Present perfect statement	Time expression
I have gone to Dr. Jenks	**for** ten years.
She has been in the same office	**since** 1999.
Ali has not had a cold	**for** several years.
We have not taken any medicine	**since** Monday.

- Use **for** when an action continued for a certain amount of time.
- Use **since** when an action began at a specific time.

A Choose the correct word.

	for	since
EXAMPLE: I've been worried about this rash ___ a week.	●	○
1. Ali's had allergies ___ he was five years old.	○	○
2. They've felt depressed ___ two months.	○	○
3. My sister's had a fever ___ last night.	○	○
4. My feet have felt better ___ I saw the podiatrist.	○	○
5. I've felt dizzy ___ a couple of days now.	○	○
6. We've seen the dermatologist twice ___ Peter got sick.	○	○
7. My sister has been pregnant ___ February.	○	○
8. Her eyes have been itchy ___ several days.	○	○

B Use the words to write present perfect sentences. Use *for* or *since* in each sentence.

EXAMPLE: Question: Julie / have high blood pressure / 1997
_**Has Julie had high blood pressure since 1997?**_____

1. Statement: I / go to the same doctor / ten years
_____

2. Statement: she / not have a vacation / last summer
_____

3. Question: Peter / gain weight / September
_____

4. Statement: my feet / hurt / several months
_____

5. Statement: they / exercise every day / 1999
_____

6. Question: you / smoke / many years
_____

7. Question: your friends / be sick / a long time
_____

CHALLENGE 4 ▶ *How long* questions

How long	*Have*	*Subject*	*Past participle*		*Time*
How long	have	you	taken	vitamins?	For two years.
How long	has	Ali	had	that rash?	Since Tuesday.
How long	has	that fish	been	in the refrigerator?	For a week.

• **How long** questions ask about the amount of time an action has continued.

A Use the words to make present perfect questions with *How long.*

EXAMPLE: you / do yoga   *How long have you done yoga?*

1. the children / be sick   _____

2. Peter / exercise   _____

3. you / know the doctor   _____

4. Maria / play tennis   _____

5. we / lift weights   _____

6. he / have high blood pressure   _____

7. they / have the flu   _____

8. your skin / be itchy   _____

9. your son / feel dizzy   _____

10. your toe / hurt   _____

B Read the answers and write the questions.

EXAMPLE: Q: *How long have you had an earache?*
               A: I've had an earache for a week.

1. Q: _____
    A: Her back has hurt since last weekend.

2. Q: _____
    A: They've known about her diabetes since February.

3. Q: _____
    A: He's had the fever for several hours.

4. Q: _____
    A: My throat has been sore since Monday.

5. Q: _____
    A: I've felt tired all week.

6. Q: _____
    A: We've been worried about our son for a month.

7. Q: _____
    A: They've had asthma for years.

8. Q: _____
    A: I've taken medication since 1998.

CHALLENGE 5 ▶ Separable and inseparable phrasal verbs

	Subject	Verb	Noun/Pronoun	Preposition	Noun
SEPARABLE PHRASAL VERBS	The doctor The doctor The doctor	**looked** **looked** **looked**	 the information it	**up** **up.** **up.**	the information.
INSEPARABLE PHRASAL VERBS	The nurse	**talked**		**to**	Anna.

- A phrasal verb consists of verb + preposition.
- A noun or pronoun can separate the parts of separable phrasal verbs.
- If a pronoun is used, a separable phrasal verb must be separated.
- A noun or pronoun cannot separate the parts of inseparable phrasal verbs.

 A Look at the phrasal verbs in the box. Then cross out the incorrect sentences below. Sometimes both sentences are correct.

Separable	look up	call up	leave out	call back	write down
Inseparable	look after	look into	get over		

EXAMPLE: Darla got over her cold in a week. / ~~She got it over in a week.~~

1. Anna called up the doctor. / Anna called the doctor up.
2. She called back the doctor at 2:00. / She called him back at 2:00.
3. He looked up the word in a dictionary. / He looked it up in a dictionary.
4. He said they would look into the problem. / He said they would look the problem into.
5. Anna wrote down all the information. / Anna wrote it down.
6. She didn't leave out anything. / She didn't leave anything out.
7. Her sister will look Anna after. / Her sister will look after Anna.
8. Anna will get over the cold in a week. / Anna will get it over in a week.

B If possible, rewrite each sentence two different ways. Rewrite sentences with inseparable phrasal verbs only once.

EXAMPLE: We called up our friends Sunday night.
  ___*We called our friends up Sunday night.*___   ___*We called them up Sunday night.*___

1. I left out my telephone number on the form.

    _____   _____

2. Dr. Santos is looking into the cause of her allergy.

    _____   _____

3. The doctor wrote down my medications.

    _____   _____

4. We looked up the number in the phone book.

    _____   _____

5. Let's call back Maria.

    _____   _____

CHALLENGE 6 ▶ Imperatives

Imperative	Use
Take this medication with water. **Don't take** it with a meal.	To give instructions or warnings
Have a nice day. **Don't worry.**	In certain polite conversational expressions

- Use the base form to make the imperative.
- A negative imperative is **do not** (**don't**) + base form.

A **Write a letter in each blank to complete each imperative correctly.**

EXAMPLE: You have a cold. Get __g__.

1. Your bones are not strong. Eat ____.
2. You are too tense. Take ____.
3. You seem very nervous. Relax ____.
4. Always stretch ____.
5. You have a cavity. Brush ____.
6. You have heart problems. Don't eat ____.
7. If you want healthy lungs, don't ____.
8. When you go in the sun, put on ____.
9. Don't gain ____.
10. Avoid salt. Flavor ____.

a. saturated fats
b. smoke
c. more calcium
d. after every meal
e. a vacation
f. weight
g. lots of sleep
h. your food with spices
i. more
j. before exercising
k. sunscreen

B **Respond with an imperative or a negative imperative. Use the verbs in the box.**

eat	keep	do	stop	work	have	sit	choose	see	cook	get

EXAMPLE: A: How can I eat better?
          B: ___**Don't choose**___ high-fat foods.

1. A: My carrots never taste fresh.
   B: _____ them in the refrigerator.

2. A: Is exercise good for me?
   B: Yes. _____ it regularly.

3. A: I want to run faster.
   B: _____ smoking.

4. A: I want to stay healthy.
   B: _____ the doctor regularly.

5. A: How can I avoid toothaches?
   B: _____ candy.

6. A: I want to get vitamins from my vegetables.
   B: _____ them too much.

7. A: I feel dizzy.
   B: _____ down.

8. A: Well, I'm off to the office.
   B: _____ too hard.

9. A: I'm always tired.
   B: _____ more rest.

10. A: Bye now.
    B: Bye. _____ a nice day.

CHALLENGE 7 ▶ More modals and related expressions

Example	Explanations
You **must** see a doctor. (You're very sick.)	**Must** shows that something is necessary.
You **must not** take penicillin. (You're allergic to it.)	**Must not** shows prohibition; something is against the law or dangerous.
He **should not** eat so much. (He'll get fat.)	Use **should** and **should not** to give advice.
We **had better not** be late for our appointment. (The doctor might not wait for us.)	Use **had better not** to give warnings.
He's **not supposed to** leave until 5:00. (All doctors have to work until 5:00.)	Use **supposed to** and **not supposed to** to tell other people about a rule.

• Modals and related expressions are followed by the base form of the verb.

A Write *a, b, c,* or *d* in the blank to show how the modal or expression is used.

a. to show necessity or prohibition   **b.** to give advice   **c.** to give a warning   **d.** to tell people about a rule

EXAMPLE: _d_ You're supposed to take your vitamins every day.

1. _____ You'd better not smoke or you'll get sick.
2. _____ I think you should exercise more.
3. _____ Your blood pressure is too high. You must learn to relax.
4. _____ You're not supposed to take the towels when you go home from the hospital.
5. _____ You should probably go on a diet.
6. _____ Your lungs are terrible. You must stop smoking.
7. _____ You had better not forget to take your medication if you want to get well.
8. _____ You must not drive a car. You might have a seizure.

B Answer each question using the modals and the words in parentheses.

EXAMPLE: Q: Can I go home now? (no / had better not)
            A: _**No, you had better not go home now.**_

1. Can we visit Darla yet? (no / not supposed to)

   _____

2. Can I take your medication? (no / must not)

   _____

3. Can Ali eat lots of fresh vegetables? (yes / should)

   _____

4. Can I call after 9:00 P.M.? (no / not supposed to call)

   _____

5. Can I start smoking again? (no / had better not)

   _____

6. Can my pregnant sister drink beer? (no / must not)

   _____

CHALLENGE 8 ▶ Future conditional statements

Cause: *if* + present tense	Effect: *will* + base form
If you smoke,	you **will get** lung cancer.
If you don't exercise,	you **will gain** weight.

- Use a future conditional statement to connect a cause and an effect.
- The **if** clause is in the present tense and the effect clause is in the future tense.
- Use a comma after the **if** clause when it comes first.
    If you exercise every day, you will develop strong muscles.
- Do not use a comma when the **if** clause comes second.
    You will develop strong muscles **if** you exercise every day.

A Correct the error in each sentence.

                                                        eats
EXAMPLE: She will develop diabetes if she ~~will eat~~ too much sugar.

1. If Ali becomes a dentist, he makes a lot of money.

2. Paulo will hurt his ankle if he will run too far.

3. Peter will gain weight if he will eat large servings of food at every meal.

4. If you will be an obstetrician, you will work with mothers and babies.

5. If you exercise every day, it benefits your circulatory system.

6. If you will be in a good mood, your blood pressure won't be too high.

7. If you visit the dentist, she checks your teeth.

8. You will be healthy if you will eat enough fiber.

B Fill in the blank with the correct tense of the verb in parentheses.

EXAMPLE: If you (see) _____**see**_____ a psychiatrist, he (ask) _____**will ask**_____ why you are unhappy.

1. You (see) _____ a lot of children if you (become) _____ a pediatrician.

2. If you (run) _____ every day, you (develop) _____ endurance.

3. You (lower) _____ your blood pressure if you (exercise) _____ regularly.

4. You (increase) _____ the flexibility of your joints if you (stretch) _____ .

5. If you (see) _____ the dermatologist, he (look) _____ at your rash.

6. You (have) _____ difficulty running if you (have) _____ asthma.

7. If you (have) _____ a stroke, you (need) _____ to go to the hospital.

8. You (get) _____ an ulcer if you (worry) _____ too much.

UNIT 6 Getting Hired

CHALLENGE 1 ► Verb + gerund form vs. verb + infinitive form

Example	Explanation
I **like working** with people. I **like to work** with people.	Some verbs can be followed by either a gerund or an infinitive with no difference in meaning.
1. I **stopped answering** the phone at noon. 2. I **stopped to answer** the phone at noon.	After the verbs **stop** and **remember**, the meaning of a gerund is different from the meaning of an infinitive. Sentence 1 means, "I didn't answer the phone after noon." Sentence 2 means, "I stopped doing something else and answered the phone at noon."
I often **go shopping** on my lunch hour.	**Go** + gerund is used in many idiomatic expressions.

- Other verbs followed by a gerund or an infinitive with no change in meaning: **begin, can't stand, continue, hate, like, love, prefer, start.**
- Other verbs followed by a gerund or an infinitive with a change in meaning: **forget** and **try.**
- Other idiomatic expressions with **go** + gerund: **go dancing, go jogging, go sightseeing, go swimming, go job hunting.**

A Match the sentences that have the same meaning.

EXAMPLE: __c__ She continued to drive after she turned 65.

1. ____ I stopped to see my sister after work.
2. ____ She will go job hunting tomorrow.
3. ____ I didn't remember to organize my desk.
4. ____ I didn't remember to fix the copier.
5. ____ She started driving at age 65.
6. ____ I stopped seeing my sister after work.
7. ____ I didn't remember fixing the copier.
8. ____ I didn't remember organizing my desk.

a. I organized my desk, but I forgot I did it.
b. I forgot to fix the copier.
c. She didn't stop driving at age 65.
d. I fixed the copier and then forgot I did it.
e. She will look for a new job tomorrow.
f. I visited my sister after work.
g. She didn't start to drive until she was 65.
h. I no longer see my sister after work.
i. I forgot to organize my desk.

B Complete each sentence with the correct infinitive or gerund. Sometimes both are correct.

to talk/talking   ~~to leave/leaving~~   to shop/shopping   to go / going   to work/working
to pay/paying   to greet/greeting   to ask/asking   to read/reading

EXAMPLE: Ramona left her references. She didn't remember _____**leaving**_____ her references.

1. Claude bought some things on his lunch hour. He went _____.
2. I didn't pay attention after five minutes. I stopped _____ attention after five minutes.
3. Kim rested from her work for a minute. She stopped _____ for a minute.
4. Kim didn't ask about the salary. She didn't remember _____ about the salary.
5. I enjoy sightseeing. I like _____ sightseeing.
6. Kyung forgot that he read about the benefits. He didn't remember _____ about benefits.
7. Kyung talked a lot about himself. He continued _____ about himself
8. Ramona didn't greet the interviewer. She didn't remember _____ him.

Used to + base form vs. be used to + gerund

CHALLENGE 2 ► *Used to* + base form vs. *be used to* + gerund

Example	Explanation
I **used to work** for Data Computers.	**Used to** + base form describes a repeated action in the past or a situation that existed in the past.
I **am used to working** with computers.	**Be used to** + gerund describes an action or a situation that has become familiar.

 A Circle *Past* if the sentence talks about a situation in the past, and *Familiar* if it talks about a situation that has become familiar.

EXAMPLE: I am used to taking the bus to work.   Past   (Familiar)

1. My mother used to be a nurse.   Past   Familiar

2. She is used to taking care of people.   Past   Familiar

3. She used to work in a large hospital.   Past   Familiar

4. My father used to work as a security guard.   Past   Familiar

5. He used to work the night shift.   Past   Familiar

6. He is used to sleeping during the day.   Past   Familiar

7. My parents used to work very hard.   Past   Familiar

8. Now they are used to being retired.   Past   Familiar

B Complete each sentence using either the base or the gerund form of the verb in parentheses.

EXAMPLE: (eat) I used to _____**eat**_____ lunch with my co-workers.

1. (work) I used to _____ in an office. Now I work at home.

2. (wake up) I used to _____ at 7:00. Now I can wake up later.

3. (wake up) I am so used to _____ at 7:00 that I can't sleep later.

4. (take) I used to _____ the subway every morning. Now I never take the subway.

5. (hear) I am used to _____ phones ringing. It's strange to be in a quiet house.

6. (see) I am used to _____ many people during the day. It's a little lonely at home.

7. (wear) I used to _____ a dress every day. Now I wear jeans.

8. (have) I am already used to _____ less stress in my day.

CHALLENGE 3 ▸ Adjective + preposition + gerund (or noun)

Subject	Verb	Adjective	Preposition	Gerund/Noun	
I	am	happy	about	**getting**	a new job.
She	is	good	at	**fixing**	machines.
They	are	interested	in	**computers.**	
He	is	afraid	of	**not having**	enough experience.

- A gerund or a noun follows an adjective + preposition.
- Other examples of adjective + preposition: **tired of, bad at, worried about.**
- To make the gerund negative, put **not** before the gerund.

A **Complete each sentence with a gerund. Use the verbs in the box.**

EXAMPLE: Claude isn't good at _____ _**answering**_ _____ math questions.

1. We are tired of _____ new workers.

2. The boss is bad at _____ the benefits program.

3. We are happy about not _____ laid off.

4. She isn't good at _____ on time.

5. Lance is afraid of _____ his job.

6. They are worried about _____ decisions.

```
train
be
lose
answer
make
explain
arrive
```

B **Write a new sentence using *adjective + preposition + gerund*.**

EXAMPLE: She writes letters very well. _**She is good at writing letters.**_

1. Learning new skills make him happy.

   _____

2. He may become a landscaper. That's his strongest interest.

   _____

3. She doesn't like to use electric tools. She's afraid of them.

   _____

4. Ramona doesn't want to lose her job. She's worried.

   _____

5. She doesn't know how to operate machines. She doesn't do it well.

   _____

6. I'm tired. I don't want to explain my decisions.

   _____

UNIT 6 Getting Hired

CHALLENGE 4 ▶ Present perfect continuous

Subject	*Have/Has*	*Been*	Present participle	
I	**have**	**been**	**working**	here for six months.
She	**has**	**been**	**receiving**	benefits since May.
You	**have**	**been**	**doing**	a good job.

- The present perfect and the present perfect continuous mean almost the same thing.
- If the action is happening at this very minute, it is better to use the present perfect continuous, *not* the present perfect: I **have been waiting** for you since noon. *Not* I **have waited** for you since noon.
- Do not use the continuous form with non-action verbs such as: **like, love, have, want, know, own, hear, see, seem,** and **understand.**

A **Complete the sentences using the present perfect continuous.**

EXAMPLE: (repair) The custodian _____**has been repairing**_____ my door since 9:00.

1. (drive) Postal workers _____ trucks for many years.
2. (count) The clerks _____ money all morning.
3. (use) Auto technicians _____ special computers for years.
4. (help) The administrative assistant _____ the manager a lot today.
5. (learn) The machine operator _____ how to repair her machine.
6. (take care of) The babysitter _____ a couple extra children this week.
7. (clean) The dental hygienist _____ people's teeth all afternoon.
8. (take) I _____ short lunch breaks this week.
9. (balance) The bookkeeper _____ accounts this week.
10. (order) My assistant _____ supplies for the whole department.

B **Circle the correct verb form.**

EXAMPLE: I ((have liked) / have been liking) working at the hospital.

1. I (have helped / have been helping) the same customer for over half an hour.
2. She (has known / has been knowing) how to type since she was 16.
3. The manager (has stood / has been standing) next to your desk for the last ten minutes.
4. He (has heard / has been hearing) the phone ring several times since noon.
5. I (have owned / have been owning) my own house for years.
6. The graphic artist (has worked on / has been working on) the same picture for an hour.
7. The photographer (has taken / has been taking) pictures all morning and he's taking mine now.
8. The boss (has seemed / has been seeming) more thoughtful lately.

44 UNIT 6

CHALLENGE 5 ► Participles used as adjectives to describe feelings

Example	Explanation
The manager offered us **disappointing** salaries.	A present participle used as an adjective often shows that the noun it describes *caused* the feeling. The salaries caused feelings of disappointment.
There were several **disappointed** people in the room.	A past participle used as an adjective shows that the noun it describes *received* the feeling. The people received a feeling of disappointment.

- Present participles are verbs that end in -**ing.**
- A past participle is the third form of the verb and usually ends in -**ed** or -**en.**

A Complete each sentence with a present participle or a past participle. Use the verbs in the box. Use each verb twice.

EXAMPLE: A. Driving a taxi is _____ ***boring*** _____ work.
　　　　　　B. Taxi drivers often feel _____ ***bored*** _____ .

1. A. A firefighter's job is often very _____ .
   B. People are usually _____ when they see a fire.
2. A. Teachers are usually _____ people.
   B. When my teacher listens carefully to what I say, I feel _____ .
3. A. If I interview and don't get the job, I will feel _____ .
   B. I will tell my friends it was a _____ interview.
4. A. The interviewer asked a lot of _____ questions.
   B. I was _____ by the questions.
5. A. It was an _____ meeting.
   B. I was _____ in everything I heard.

~~bore~~
interest
understand
frighten
confuse
disappoint

B Circle the correct participle.

EXAMPLE: If your job bores you, you feel (boring /(bored)).

1. After you finish work for the day, you feel (relaxing / relaxed).
2. If you love your work, your job is probably (interesting / interested).
3. Mechanics are often (tiring / tired) after working eight hours.
4. When I got a $25 raise, I was (surprising / surprised).
5. If you know of a good job for me, I am (interesting / interested).
6. Taking messages can be (boring / bored) work.
7. Some taxi drivers make a (surprising / surprised) amount of money.
8. Cooking in a restaurant makes me feel (tiring / tired).

CHALLENGE 6 ▶ Adverbs of manner

Adjective	Adverb	Explanation
He's a careful worker.	He works **carefully.**	You can form most adverbs by adding **-ly** to the end of an adjective.
She is a confident driver at all times.	She drives her car **confidently** at all times.	Adverbs of manner usually follow the verb.
He is a very quick learner.	He learns very **quickly.**	You can use **very** before an adverb of manner.
She is a hard worker.	She works **hard.**	Some adjectives and adverbs have the same form: **fast, late, hard.**

A Write the correct adjective or adverb in each sentence.

EXAMPLE: (honest) Claude answers questions _____ ***honestly*** _____.

He is an _____ ***honest*** _____ person.

1. (careful) Kim is a _____ worker.

   She operates her machine _____.

2. (intelligent) Ramona is very _____.

   She speaks _____.

3. (hard) Kyung works _____.

   He's a very _____ worker.

4. (enthusiastic) He is an _____ employee.

   He does his job _____.

5. (warm) The receptionist greets people _____.

   She has a _____ personality.

B Use the words to write sentences. Use the correct adverb form and word order.

EXAMPLE: (sensitive) Lance / ask / questions   ***Lance asks questions sensitively.***

1. (quick) Kim / learn / her job   _____

2. (careful) we / fill out / the forms   _____

3. (fast) I / learn / my duties   _____

4. (arrogant) he / speak / to the secretary _____

5. (honest) Claude / handle money   _____

6. (thoughtful) she / answer questions   _____

7. (late) Ray / work / at the restaurant   _____

8. (slow) we / dialed the number   _____

CHALLENGE 7 ▷ Noun clauses

Example	Explanation
I think **that bookkeeping is a good job.**	A noun clause can follow certain verbs that describe thinking.
I am surprised **that it pays so little.**	A noun clause can follow **be** + certain adjectives.

- Verbs that describe thinking include: **believe, expect, feel, forget, hope, know, realize, remember, think,** and **understand.**
- Adjectives that come after **be** and can be followed by noun clauses include: **certain, clear, glad, happy, sure, surprised,** and **worried.**
- **That** can be omitted from most sentences containing a noun clause.

A **Write correct sentences with noun clauses. Use words from each column.**

everyone knows
the custodian realizes
I forgot
the receptionist understands
a graphic artist knows
salespeople know
teachers understand
the administrative assistant knows
the mechanic believes

color is a powerful tool
I should show the interviewer my resume
students sometimes get tired
computers are necessary in banks
that he can fix your car
he will have to work the night shift
he should answer the phones quickly
that she will be working with the boss
that the customer is always right

EXAMPLE: *Everyone knows that computers are necessary in banks.*

1. _____
2. _____
3. _____
4. _____
5. _____
6. _____
7. _____
8. _____

B **Use the words to write sentences with *be* + adjective + noun clause.**

EXAMPLE: Lance / happy / he has a new secretary   *Lance is happy that he has a new secretary.*

1. we / worried / bookkeeper may be dishonest   _____
2. Ramona / sure / she can take care of six children   _____
3. it / clear / children shouldn't operate machines   _____
4. I / glad / I speak several languages   _____
5. we / surprised / Lance can sew   _____
6. Claude / happy / the taxi driver can read maps   _____
7. the hygienist / glad / I was early   _____

UNIT
6 | **Getting Hired**

CHALLENGE 8 ► *Would rather*

	Would	Subject	*Rather*	Base form	*Or*	Base form
QUESTIONS	**Would**	Kim	**rather**	type	or	answer phones?
	Would	You	**rather**	work days	or	(work) nights?
	Subject	*Would rather*	Base form	*Than*	Base form	
STATEMENTS	She	**would rather**	answer phones	than	type.	
	I	**'d rather**	work days	than	nights.	

- **Or** is used between the choices in a question.
- **Than** is used between the choices in a statement.
- The second verb in questions and statements can be omitted if it is the same as the first.
- **Would** is often contracted to **'d** in statements: **I'd, you'd, he'd, she'd, we'd, they'd.**

A Unscramble the words to make questions and statements with *would rather.*

EXAMPLE: (question) in an office in a school you rather work or would
__Would you rather work in an office or in a school?__

1. (statement) take a class study at home than she'd rather

   _____

2. (statement) use computers repair computers they'd than rather

   _____

3. (question) balance accounts talk to customers or she rather would

   _____

4. (question) drive a truck a bus or you would rather

   _____

B Write questions and answers with *would rather.* Use *than* in the answers.

EXAMPLE: the bookkeeper / have old computer / new computer (he / new)
   Q: *__Would the bookkeeper rather have an old computer or a new computer?__*
   A: *__He'd rather have a new computer than an old computer.__*

1. you / walk / take a taxi (walk)
   Q: _____
   A: _____
2. he / finish the report / go home (go home)
   Q: _____
   A: _____
3. Kyung / read reports / answer the phone (answer the phone)
   Q: _____
   A: _____
4. you / be a programmer / be a technician (be a programmer)
   Q: _____
   A: _____

Would rather

CHALLENGE 1 ▶ Possessive adjectives and possessive pronouns

	Possessive	Example	Explanation
ADJECTIVES	my, your, his, her, our, their	**My** pay is $500 a week.	Possessive adjectives come before a noun and show possession.
PRONOUNS	mine, yours, his, hers, ours, theirs	**Yours** is $450 a week.	Possessive pronouns take the place of a noun and show possession.

• A noun never comes after a possessive pronoun: **Mine** ~~office~~ is clean.

A Circle the correct possessive form.

EXAMPLE: She works the day shift. ((Her)/ Hers) hours are 9:00 to 5:00.

1. My net pay is $936. (Her / Hers) is $1000.
2. His paycheck was late. (My / Mine) was on time.
3. They didn't give me my paycheck yet. Did you get (your / yours) check?
4. My tax deductions are very high, but (your / yours) aren't.
5. Their company pays for disability insurance, but (my / mine) company doesn't.
6. Your gross pay is more than (my / mine).
7. This is my pay stub. Where's (your / yours) stub?
8. His hourly wage isn't as good as (their / theirs).

B Rewrite the second sentence. Use a possessive adjective or possessive pronoun to replace the underlined phrase.

EXAMPLE: My pay is $7.50 an hour. How much <u>do you make</u>?
(possessive pronoun) ___*How much is yours?*_____

1. My deductions are over 30% of my pay. How much <u>do you pay</u>?
(possessive adjective) _____
2. Fred makes about $400 a month. <u>Fred's</u> sister makes about $900 a month.
(possessive adjective) _____
3. So's company pays for Medicare. <u>The company I work for</u> doesn't pay for it.
(possessive pronoun) _____
4. Susan's co-workers are friendly. <u>The people I work with</u> aren't.
(possessive pronoun) _____
5. Alexander's net pay goes up every year. <u>The amount you get paid</u> doesn't go up.
(possessive adjective) _____
6. My tax payments are high. <u>The payments you make</u> are lower.
(possessive pronoun) _____
7. You and I get paychecks more often than Ellen. <u>Ellen's paychecks</u> come only once a month.
(possessive pronoun) _____

CHALLENGE 2 ▶ *Could, might, ought to,* and *have to*

Example	Explanation
You **could** have an accident. You **might** get hurt.	**Could** and **might** show there is a chance that something will happen in the future.
You look tired. You **ought to** go home. You **ought to** wear your seat belt all the time.	Use **ought to** to give advice and to show there is one correct way to do something.
You **have to** lock the door when you leave.	Use **have to** to show that something is necessary.

A Write *a, b, c,* or *d* in the blank to show how the modal or expression is used.

a. to show there is a chance something will happen
b. to give advice
c. to show there is one correct way to do something
d. to show that something is necessary

EXAMPLE: __*b*__ You ought to take family leave when the baby is born.

1. _____ Don't smoke in the storeroom. It could start a fire.
2. _____ You have to take shorter breaks.
3. _____ The smaller boxes ought to go on top of the bigger boxes.
4. _____ Everyone has to pay taxes.
5. _____ You might get a raise if you work hard.
6. _____ You ought to arrive on time if you don't want to get in trouble.
7. _____ You have to wear shoes in the factory.
8. _____ The manager ought to pay me $14 an hour. It's in my contract.
9. _____ They might open another office down the street.
10. _____ You've worked hard. You ought to ask for a bonus.

B Circle the better modal.

EXAMPLE: It's good to have disability insurance. You (have to / (could)) get sick.

1. If you want my advice, you (might / ought to) take the new job.
2. All full-time employees (could / have to) work at least 35 hours a week.
3. I'm not sure, but I (might / have to) get a raise next month.
4. If you want to, you (could / have to) ask for a day off.
5. All part-time employees (might / have to) work less than 20 hours a week.
6. You (might / ought to) be nicer to the boss if you want a raise.
7. You (might / have to) get a raise if you're nicer to her.
8. The U.S. government (ought to / has to) give everyone free health insurance.

CHALLENGE 3 ▶ Polite requests with *Would you mind*... and *Could you*...

Request	Description
Would you mind making a copy for me?	Polite and formal
Could you look over this report?	Polite and less formal
Can you help me with this box?	Polite and informal
Give me that!	Very informal, or impolite

- **Would you mind** is followed by a gerund.
- **Can** and **could** are followed by the base form.
- Use polite and formal language when talking with a boss or manager.
- Use polite or informal language when talking with coworkers.
- Use very informal or impolite language in an emergency or to show anger.

A Label each request. Use the descriptions above.

EXAMPLE: Can you answer that phone?   *polite and informal* _____

1. Would you mind reviewing my resume again?   _____
2. Can you help me with these reports?   _____
3. Call the boss right away!   _____
4. Can you come in early tomorrow morning?   _____
5. Would you mind changing your 2:00 appointment to 3:00?   _____
6. Could you sign all three copies?   _____

B Complete the responses. Some answers can use either *can* or *could*.

EXAMPLE: (lend me your goggles) To a friend:
        Hey, Ellen.   *Can you lend me your goggles?* _____

1. (sign this check) To your supervisor:
   Oh, Ms. Reeves. _____, please?
2. (open the door) To a friend:
   Say, Jose. _____ for me?
3. (help me pick them up) To a stranger:
   Oh no! I dropped all the reports. _____
4. (answer the phones) To your co-worker:
   Oh, Arnie. _____ while I'm at lunch?
5. (open the door) To a friend:
   I'm in a hurry! _____
6. (check over this report) To your manager:
   I know you're busy, Mr. Adams, but _____
7. (sign these letters) To your company president:
   Excuse me, Mrs. Camus. _____

So...that and such...that to show results

CHALLENGE 4 ▶ *So...that* and *such...that* to show results

so + adjective + *(that)*		
Minh's report was	**so good that**	the boss gave her a raise.
The raise was	**so big that**	her taxes went up.
such a/an + adjective + noun + *(that)*		
Minh wrote	**such a good report that**	the boss gave her a raise.
She got	**such a big raise that**	her taxes when up.

• Omit **a/an** before non-count nouns.
   She had **such good health that** she never missed a day of work.

A Correct the mistakes in the sentences.

EXAMPLE: Vanessa was ~~such~~ *so* late that the boss was angry.

1. Wassim is lazy that he'll never get a promotion.

2. We worked for such long time that we were really tired.

3. Fred has such interesting resume that he got an interview right away.

4. Ellen is such friendly that the customers all love her.

5. Leticia was a good programmer that they made her a manager.

6. My co-workers are serious that they never take a break.

7. Ellen was such quiet worker that no one knew she was in the office.

8. My boss is such demanding that I have to work late every day.

B Complete the sentences using *so* or *such* expressions. Use the words in parentheses.

EXAMPLE: (relaxed) My office is _____ **so relaxed** _____ that I enjoy going there.

1. (patient) I have _____ boss that I'll never leave my job.

2. (courteous) The receptionist is _____ that the customers all mention it.

3. (reserved) The programmers are _____ that they never talk to anyone.

4. (hardworking) They are _____ employees that they all got raises.

5. (ambitious) Ellen is _____ woman that I know she'll be successful.

6. (strict) The boss is _____ that everyone is afraid of him.

7. (good) She gives _____ advice that everyone asks her for help.

8. (long) My vacation was _____ that I missed my co-workers.

CHALLENGE 5 ▶ Adjective + infinitive phrase

	Subject	*Be*	Adjective	Infinitive phrase
STATEMENTS	It	is	**important**	**to be on time.**
	Arnie	was	**sorry**	**to leave the job.**
	They	are not	**prepared**	**to learn the new system.**
	Be	Subject	Adjective	Infinitive phrase
YES/NO **QUESTIONS**	Are	you	**willing**	**to work long hours?**

• The infinitive can be used after certain adjectives: **afraid, expensive, glad, happy, important, pleased, prepared, ready, sad, sorry, surprised,** and **willing.**

A Match the two parts of each sentence.

EXAMPLE: Jose wasn't ready __*e*__

1. Wassim was afraid _____
2. We were surprised _____
3. Ellen is prepared _____
4. I am sad _____
5. Are you pleased _____
6. Is she ready _____
7. Is it important _____
8. Fred wasn't happy _____

a. to be on time every day?
b. to learn that the president made so little money.
c. to have a new boss?
d. to take on that much responsibility at age 21?
e̸. to retire at age 52.
f. to move to a smaller office.
g. to hear that my co-workers are leaving.
h. to ask for a raise because he was so reserved.
i. to leave if she doesn't get a raise.

B Use the words to make sentences with present tense *be* + adjective + infinitive phrase.

EXAMPLE: it / expensive / buy all new computers
(statement) ___*It's expensive to buy all new computers.*___

1. Susan / not ready / become a manager
   (statement) _____
2. we / prepared / hire six new people
   (question) _____
3. he / not willing / learn French
   (statement) _____
4. Alex / pleased / change his hours
   (statement) _____
5. you / sorry / be leaving
   (question) _____
6. I / not happy / hear the news
   (statement) _____
7. she / glad / change jobs
   (question) _____

Adjective + infinitive phrase

CHALLENGE 6 ▶ *How much* and *How many*

How many	Count noun	
How many	deductions	does Fred have?
How many	sick days	did Ellen use last year?

• Use **How many** questions to ask about things that can be counted.

How much	Non-count noun	
How much	tax	does Fred pay?
	vacation	did Ellen take last year?

• Use **How much** questions to ask about things that can't be counted.

A Write the nouns in the correct column. Make the count nouns plural.

company	~~job~~	time	knowledge	pay	deduction
math	insurance	manager	proposal	employee	information

Count nouns

____jobs____ _____

_____ _____

_____ _____

Non-count nouns

_____ _____

_____ _____

_____ _____

B Write the questions using words and phrases from each column.

How many	~~English~~	did you pay this month
How much	programs	are you willing to work each week
	state tax	did you take when you broke your leg
	sick days	do we have before the meeting
	managerial experience	do we spend on office supplies every year
	overtime	~~have you studied~~
	money	do you need before you get a promotion
	goggles	do you need for your co-workers
	time	can you run on this computer

EXAMPLE: ___*How much English have you studied?*___

1. _____
2. _____
3. _____
4. _____
5. _____
6. _____
7. _____
8. _____

CHALLENGE 7 ▶ Reporting verbs

Subject	Verb	Object	Infinitive
I	**asked**	her	to finish the report. not to go to the meeting.
She	**told**	me	to work faster. not to be so slow.

Subject	Verb	Object	Preposition	Gerund/Noun
I	**thanked**	her	for	helping me. not being angry.
They	**criticized**	me	for	leaving early. not staying late.
We	**praised**	him	for	his management skills.

A **Complete the sentences with the correct form of the verb.**

EXAMPLE: She asked me ___*to*___ _____*repair*_____ the machine.

smoke
listen
~~repair~~
answer
make

1. I praised them _____ _____ a good contract.
2. He criticized us _____ _____ _____ carefully.
3. They told us _____ _____ _____ in the building.
4. I thanked her _____ _____ my messages.

B **Imagine these sentences were all said to you. Change them to reported speech using the verbs in parentheses.**

EXAMPLE: "You work very hard."
            (praise) The manager ___*praised me for working very hard.*___

1. "Please, could you read this report?"
    (ask) The supervisor _____
2. "Don't make so much noise!"
    (tell) The janitor _____
3. "You are always late!"
    (criticize) Mrs. Perkins _____
4. "You took my shift yesterday. That was nice of you."
    (thank) Alice _____
5. "You never answer your phone!"
    (criticize) The supervisor _____
6. "You did a great job at the sales conference."
    (praise) The manager _____
7. "Please don't make any more appointments for today."
    (ask) The president _____
8. "You didn't forget my packages!"
    (thank) The assistant _____

CHALLENGE 8 ▸ Three-word phrasal verbs

Subject	Three-word phrasal verb	Object	
We	**get through with**	work	at 5:00.
We	**get through with**	it	at 5:00.
We	~~get work through with~~	at 5:00.	
We	~~get through it with~~	at 5:00.	

- Three-word verbs consist of verb + preposition + preposition.
- A three-word verb always takes an object.
- A noun or pronoun object cannot separate the parts of a three-word verb.

A **Study this list of phrasal verbs. Then unscramble the sentences.**

Phrasal verb	Meaning	Phrasal verb	Meaning
get along with	be friends with	look forward to	expect something good
get rid of	remove something	make sure of	check the truth of
get through with	finish	run out of	finish the supply of
keep up with	understand everything about	take care of	be responsible for

EXAMPLE: at with through I got work 7:00   *I got through with work at 7:00.*

1. of sure please make answer the   _____
2. time card please care take of your   _____
3. with in along I everyone the office get   _____
4. of got our computers rid old we   _____
5. for of out we the copier paper ran   _____
6. I can't all up the with new keep programs   _____
7. today's to forward I'm looking meeting   _____
8. through my until won't training get with May I   _____

B **Complete the sentences with the correct three-word verb.**

EXAMPLE: We have no more application forms. We have ____*run*____ ____*out*____ ____*of*____ them.

1. When do you think we'll _____ _____ _____ this meeting?
2. I can't _____ _____ _____ all the changes in my health insurance program.
3. Tomorrow is Saturday. I always _____ _____ _____ the weekend.
4. Could you _____ _____ _____ the guests for a minute? Maybe they'd like some coffee.
5. Don't we have any pencils? Have we _____ _____ _____ them?
6. I don't always _____ _____ _____ my boss. I hope I don't lose my job.
7. Let's _____ _____ _____ this old office furniture. It looks terrible!
8. Check the numbers again. We need to _____ _____ _____ the totals.

CHALLENGE 1 ▶ Contrasts with *but* and *however*

First idea	Second idea	Statement of contrast
Rosario wants bigger schools.	Liz doesn't want bigger schools.	Rosario wants bigger schools, **but** Liz doesn't.
Dawson doesn't want smaller class sizes.	Kim wants smaller class sizes.	Dawson doesn't want smaller class sizes; **however**, Kim does.

- Use a comma before a contrasting statement that starts with **but**.
- Use a semicolon before a contrasting statement that starts with **however** and use a comma after the word **however**.
- Use only the subject and helping verb in the contrasting statement.
  This school has large classes, **but** that school doesn't ~~have large classes~~.

A Match the two parts of each sentence.

EXAMPLE: Thanksgiving is in November; __g__

1. New Jersey is in the East; ____
2. Enrico wants more parks, ____
3. Hollywood is in California, ____
4. Washington state has tall mountains; ____
5. Texas is a very large state, ____
6. Bellmore has a lot of police; ____
7. Bellmore offers job training programs, ____
8. Bellmore lowered its schools' tuition; ____

a. however, Littletown didn't.
b. however, California isn't.
c. however, Littletown doesn't.
d. however, Mississippi doesn't.
e. but Chicago isn't.
f. but Littletown doesn't.
g. but Christmas isn't.
h. but Liz doesn't.
i. but Rhode Island isn't.

B Use the words to write contrasts with *but* and *however.*

EXAMPLE: Liz has visited Texas. Ali hasn't visited Texas.
          (but) **_Liz has visited Texas, but Ali hasn't._**

1. The Statue of Liberty is in New York. The Liberty Bell isn't in New York.
   (however) _____
2. Texas is a big oil producer. Kentucky isn't a big oil producer.
   (but) _____
3. San Francisco is a major port. Hollywood isn't a major port.
   (however) _____
4. Massachusetts was a British colony. Oklahoma wasn't a British colony.
   (but) _____
5. Lincoln was assassinated. Washington wasn't assassinated.
   (but) _____
6. Labor Day is in September. Veteran's Day is not in September.
   (however) _____
7. Washington is on the dollar bill. Lincoln isn't on the dollar bill.
   (but) _____

Citizens and Community

CHALLENGE 2 ▶ Statements of agreement with *both* and *neither*

First idea	Second idea	Statement of agreement
The president is part of the executive branch.	The cabinet is part of the executive branch.	**Both** the president **and** the cabinet are part of the executive branch.
Enrico doesn't want high taxes.	Ali doesn't want high taxes.	**Neither** Enrico **nor** Ali wants high taxes.

- Use **and** in statements beginning with **both**.
- Use **nor** in statements beginning with **neither**.
- In a **both/and** statement, the verb agrees with the combined subject.
    Both Maria **and** Marco **are** citizens.
- The verb in a **neither/nor** statement agrees with the second subject.
    Neither Maria **nor** Marco **is** a citizen.

A Look at the chart about the citizens. Write *True* or *False* in front of each statement.

	Rosario	Cherie	Dawson	Suzanna
voted	No	No	Yes	No
marches in parades	No	Yes	Yes	Yes
has met the mayor	No	No	Yes	No

EXAMPLE: ___*False*___ Both Rosario and Cherie voted.

1. _____ Neither Rosario nor Cherie has met the mayor.
2. _____ Both Dawson and Suzanne march in parades.
3. _____ Both Rosario and Cherie march in parades.
4. _____ Neither Cherie nor Suzanna has met the mayor.
5. _____ Neither Suzanna nor Dawson voted.
6. _____ Both Dawson and Cherie have met the mayor.
7. _____ Neither Suzanna nor Cherie voted.
8. _____ Both Cherie and Dawson have met the mayor.

B Correct the error or errors in each sentence.

EXAMPLE: Both the secretary of state ~~nor~~ *and* the secretary of defense ~~is~~ *are* in the cabinet.

1. Neither the executive and judicial branch can make laws.
2. Both the president and the vice president lives in Washington, D.C.
3. Neither the House of Representatives nor the Senate have 600 members.
4. Neither the president nor the cabinet are part of the judicial branch.
5. Both the Senate and the House of Representatives is part of Congress.
6. Neither the executive branch and the legislative branch control immigration.
7. Both Texas and Rhode Island has two senators.
8. Neither Congress nor the cabinet prepare the budget.

UNIT
8
Citizens and Community

CHALLENGE 3 ▶ Contrary-to-fact conditionals

Possibility: *if* + subject + past tense	Possible result: *would* + base form
If we **spent** more money on education,	we **would have** better schools.
If we **didn't have** a police force,	there **would be** more crime.

- Use contrary-to-fact conditionals to describe situations that aren't true now and that the speaker thinks will probably never be true.
- Use a comma after the **if** clause when it comes first.
- In formal English, use **were** for the past tense of **be** with all subjects in the **if** clause.

A Fill in each blank with the correct tense of the verb in parentheses.

EXAMPLE: If housing prices (be) ____**were**____ lower, we (move) ____**would move**____ to a larger apartment.

1. If they (increase) _____ taxes, I (move) _____ away.

2. If they (build) _____ a new park, the children (have) _____ a better place to play.

3. If people (clean up) _____ after their dogs, the streets (look) _____ a lot better.

4. If prices (be) _____ more affordable, we (buy) _____ a house.

5. If we (have) _____ less traffic, there (be) _____ fewer accidents.

6. If the city (provide) _____ cheap housing, the community (be) _____ more diverse.

7. If the river (not be) _____ so dirty, we (swim) _____ in it.

8. If the community (have) _____ more office space, it (attract) _____ new businesses.

B Complete each sentence. Use the correct form of the verbs in the box.

have	feel	be	~~give~~	appreciate	like	improve	learn	work

EXAMPLE: If I were mayor, I ____**would give**____ more money to schools.

1. If schools _____ more money, students would have newer books.

2. If they had newer books, students _____ more interested in learning.

3. If they were more interested in learning, they _____ more.

4. If students learned more, they _____ their own intelligence.

5. If they _____ proud of themselves, they would also feel happier.

6. If students were happier, they _____ school more.

7. If they liked school more, they _____ harder.

8. If they worked harder, they _____ their grades.

UNIT 8 Citizens and Community

CHALLENGE 4 ▸ Passives—Part 1

Active	Passive (*be* + past participle)
We celebrate Veterans' Day on November 11.	Veterans' Day **is celebrated** on November 11.
Roosevelt introduced the New Deal in 1937.	The New Deal **was introduced** in 1937.

- The active voice shows that the subject of the sentence performs the action.
- The passive voice shows that the subject of the sentence receives the action.
- **Be** in a passive sentence is in the same tense as the verb in an active sentence.

A Match the two parts of each sentence.

EXAMPLE: Soldiers who died in wars __*b*__

1. Thanksgiving _____
2. Large turkey meals _____
3. The first Monday in September _____
4. The Fourth of July _____
5. The Declaration of Independence _____
6. The Liberty Bell _____
7. Dr. Martin Luther King, Jr. _____
8. Dr. Martin Luther King, Jr. Day _____

a. is celebrated with fireworks.
b. are remembered on Veteran's Day.
c. was chosen as the date for Labor Day.
d. is found in Philadelphia.
e. is celebrated in November.
f. was assassinated in 1968.
g. was first celebrated in 1986.
h. are eaten on Thanksgiving.
i. was signed in Philadelphia.

B Circle the correct verb form in each sentence.

EXAMPLE: Roosevelt (remembers / (is remembered)) for the New Deal.

1. Many soldiers (killed / were killed) in the Revolutionary War.
2. Congress (signed / was signed) the Declaration of Independence in 1776.
3. Presidents' Day (celebrates / is celebrated) in February.
4. Soldiers (march / are marched) in Veterans' Day parades.
5. Flags (carry / are carried) in the parade.
6. Native Americans (taught / were taught) Americans how to plant corn.
7. Native Americans (invited / were invited) to the first Thanksgiving.
8. The Pilgrims (came / were come) from Europe.
9. Dr. Martin Luther King, Jr. (fought / was fought) for civil rights.
10. Dr. King's achievements (remember / are remembered) today.

UNIT 8 — Citizens and Community

CHALLENGE 5 ▶ Passives—Part 2

Active	Passive (*be* + past participle)
The Supreme Court justice **is making** a judgment.	A judgment **is being made**.
Congress **will make** some new laws.	Some new laws **will be made**.
The president **has signed** several new laws.	Several new laws **have been signed**.
Americans **can reelect** the president only once.	The president **can be reelected** only once.

- Note the use of present continuous, future, present perfect, and modals in the active and passive pairs.
- The performer of the action can be included in a passive sentences after the word **by**.
  Several new laws **have been signed by** the president.

A Use the correct form of the verb in parentheses to complete the sentences.

EXAMPLE: (divide) The power of the U.S. government is _____**divided**_____ among three branches.

1. (balance) The power of the executive branch is _____ by the judicial branch.
2. (govern) The United States has been _____ by the Constitution since 1791.
3. (make) New laws are being _____ every year.
4. (reelect) Many people think the current president will be _____.
5. (chose) The cabinet is _____ by the president.
6. (include) A new secretary of education will be _____ in the cabinet.
7. (declare) War has been _____ several times in U.S. history.
8. (collect) Taxes are being _____ electronically now.

B Rewrite each sentence in passive form. Use *by* to tell who performs the action.

EXAMPLE: The people elect the mayor. _**The mayor is elected by the people.**_

1. A committee will count the votes.

   _____

2. The superintendent of schools runs the school system.

   _____

3. The teachers are making some important decisions.

   _____

4. This year the mayor has raised the school budget.

   _____

5. The mayor is suggesting a million-dollar budget.

   _____

6. The tax assessor sets school tax rates.

   _____

7. The teachers support the mayor.

   _____

Be + adjective + infinitive *(side tab)*

CHALLENGE 6 ▶ *Be* + adjective + infinitive

Subject	*Be*	Adjective	Infinitive	
It	is	difficult	to find	affordable rents.
It	will be	impossible	to buy	a house soon.
Kim	was	lucky	to find	a cheap apartment.
She	is	ready	to move	right now.

- After the word **it,** the following adjectives can be used: **dangerous, difficult, easy, good, hard, important, possible, necessary, fun, expensive, impossible.**
- After names or subject pronouns, the following adjectives can be used: **afraid, glad, happy, lucky, prepared, proud, ready, sad.**

A   Use the words to write sentences using *be* + adjective + infinitive.

EXAMPLE: it / fun / look at / new apartments
(present) ___*It's fun to look at new apartments.*___

1. Ali / glad / see / all the ads in the newspaper
(past) _____

2. it / possible / find / a nice place for $800
(present) _____

3. Ali / prepared / pay / $1000 a month
(present) _____

4. it / not easy / afford / the rent
(future) _____

5. he / be / happy / move out of / his old apartment
(future) _____

6. his roommates / sad / see / him leave
(past) _____

B   Complete the sentences. Use a word from each box.

| afraid   ~~dangerous~~   proud   expensive |
| important   easy   impossible   difficult   good |

| have   drive   do   bring   look |
| get   ~~walk~~   save   build |

EXAMPLE: It is ___*dangerous*___ ___*to walk*___ in the street.

1. I am _____ _____ so close to the cars.
2. It is _____ _____ where you are going.
3. It will be _____ _____ new sidewalks.
4. But it is _____ _____ new sidewalks.
5. It is _____ _____ enough money for a car.
6. I will be _____ _____ a new car.
7. With a new car, it will be _____ _____ my grocery shopping.
8. In the past, it was _____ _____ home more than two bags of food.

UNIT 8 | **Citizens and Community**

CHALLENGE 7 ▸ Causatives with *make* and *have*

Subject	*Make/Have*	Object	Base form	
The mayor	made	the citizens	pay	higher taxes.
The police officer	makes	us	cross	at the corner.
The mayor	has	visitors	sit	in the back.
The city council	had	some teenagers	clean up	the river.

- Causative verbs show that the subject causes the object to do something.
- **Make** shows that the subject forces the object to do something.
- **Have** shows that the subject gives the object a job to do.

A **Unscramble the words to make sentences.**

EXAMPLE: work / begin / his / mayor / staff / at / 7:00 A.M. / the / makes
  **The mayor makes his staff begin work at 7:00 A.M.**

1. meetings / attend / makes / all / mayor / staff / the / his

   _____

2. mail / he / assistant / has / open / his / his

   _____

3. has / he / driver / his / take / to / morning / town hall / every / him

   _____

4. in / the / visitors / has / he / waiting room / wait

   _____

5. coffee / secretary / his / bring / has / them / he

   _____

6. people / he / identification / leave / building / makes / without / the

   _____

B **Choose the best word in parentheses to complete each sentence.**

EXAMPLE: My boss (has / (makes)) us work on some national holidays!

1. I (had / made) the taxi driver take me to the Statue of Liberty.
2. We (have / make) the post office forward our mail.
3. The bank robber (had / made) the bank teller hand over the money.
4. The police officer (had / made) the drunk driver pull over.
5. She (had / made) the hairstylist dye her hair blonde.
6. The customs officials (had / made) me show them my passport.
7. Mario (has / makes) his father send him his hometown newspaper a few times a month.
8. Rosa is upset that her mother (has / makes) her come home by 10:00 each night.

Causatives with *make* and *have*

UNIT 8 **63**

UNIT 8 | Citizens and Community

CHALLENGE 8 ▶ Reported speech

Direct speech	Reported speech
The city clerk said, "I **am feeling** really tired."	She said she **was feeling** really tired.
She said, "I **need** a vacation."	She said she **needed** a vacation.
She said, "I **fell** asleep at my desk."	She said she **had fallen** asleep at her desk.
She said, "I **will return** in two weeks."	She said she **would return** in two weeks.

• In reported speech the verb tenses change to the past of the direct speech form.
    simple present → simple past   present continuous → past continuous
    simple → past perfect   modal **will** → modal **would**
• Subject pronouns also change in reported speech.
• In reported speech, quotation marks are not used and there is no comma after **said.**

A Rewrite the sentences as reported speech.

EXAMPLE: The students said, "Room 16 is too small."   ***They said room 16 was too small.***

1. They said, "We are sitting too close together." _____
2. They said, "We feel uncomfortable." _____
3. They said, "We won't be able to study." _____
4. They said, "We are hoping to change rooms." _____
5. They said, "We liked room 12 last term." _____
6. They said, "Room 12 was much larger." _____
7. They said, "We will talk to the principal." _____
8. They said, "He will understand." _____

B Rewrite each sentence as reported speech.

Kim Vo said, "I am running for mayor. (1) I know exactly what to do. (2) But I will need the help of all voters. (3) I won't be able to do it alone. (4) I talked to the superintendent of schools. (5) He promised to cooperate."

The superintendent said: (6) "The last mayor didn't support the school system. (7) I need more money to run the schools. (8) I don't want to disappoint students and parents. (9) I will try to make a lot of improvements. (10) I am going to need everyone's support."

EXAMPLE: Kim Vo said ***she was running for mayor.***

1. She said _____
2. She said _____
3. She said _____
4. She said _____
5. She said _____
6. The superintendent said _____
7. He said _____
8. He said _____
9. He said _____
10. He said _____

APPENDIX

► GLOSSARY OF GRAMMAR TERMS

adjective	a word that describes a noun (Example: the _red_ hat)
adverb	a word that modifies a verb, adjective, or another adverb (Example: She eats _quickly_.)
affirmative	not negative and not a question (Example: _I like him._)
animate/inanimate	objects that have action or motion (Example: _teacher_ or _water_) / objects that don't act or move (Example: _book_ or _desk_)
apostrophe	a punctuation mark that shows missing letters in contractions or possession (Example: _It's_ or _Jim's_)
article	words used before a noun (Example: _a_, _an_, _the_)
base form	the main form of the verb, used without _to_ (Example: _be, have, study_)
causative	a verb form that indicates that the subject of the sentence causes the object to do something (Example: I _made_ her study.)
clause	a group of words that has a subject and a verb (Example: We live here.)
comma	the punctuation mark (,) used to indicate a pause or separation (Example: I live in an apartment, and you live in a house.)
comparative	a form of an adjective, adverb, or noun that expresses the difference between two or more things (Example: My sister is _taller_ than you.)
complement	a word or words that add to or complete an idea after the verb (Example: He is _happy_.)
conditional, contrary to fact	a structure used for talking about an imaginary situation that is not true at the present time (Example: If I won the lottery, I _would buy_ a mansion.)
conditional, future	a structure used for talking about possibilities in the future (Example: If it rains, I _will bring_ an umbrella.)
conjugation	the forms of a verb (Example: I _am_, You _are_, We _are_, They _are_, He _is_, She _is_, It _is_)
conjunction	a type of word that joins other words or phrases (Example: Maria _and_ Gilberto)
consonant	any letter of the alphabet that is not a vowel (Example: b, c, d, f...)
continuous form	a verb form that expresses action during time (Example: He _is shopping._)
contraction	shortening of a word, syllable, or word group by omission of a sound or letter (Example: It is = _It's_, does not = _doesn't_)
count nouns	nouns that can be counted by number (Example: one _apple_, two _apples_)
definite article	use of _the_ when a noun is known to speaker and listener (Example: I know _the_ store.)
exclamation mark	a punctuation symbol marking surprise or emotion (Example: Hello_!_)

formal	polite or respectful language (Example: *Could* you *please* give me that?)
future	a verb form in the future tense (Example: I <u>*will study*</u> at that school next year.)
gerund	an -*ing* form of a verb that functions as a noun (Example: <u>*Swimming*</u> is fun.)
imperative	a command form of a verb (Example: <u>*Listen!*</u> or <u>*Look out!*</u>)
indefinite article	*a* or *an* used before a noun when something is talked about for the first time or when *the* is too specific (Example: There's <u>*a*</u> new restaurant here.)
infinitive	the main form of a verb, usually used with *to* (Example: I like <u>*to run*</u> fast.)
informal	friendly or casual language (Example: <u>*Can*</u> I have that?)
irregular verb	a verb different from regular form verbs (Example: be = *am, are, is, was, were, being*)
modal auxiliary	a verb that indicates a mood (ability, possibility, etc.) and is followed by the base form of another verb (Example: I <u>*can read*</u> English well.)
modifier	a word or phrase that describes another (Example: a <u>*good*</u> friend)
negative	the opposite of affirmative (Example: She *does* <u>*not*</u> *like* meat.)
noun	a name of a person, place, or thing (Example: <u>*Joe*</u>, <u>*England*</u>, <u>*bottle*</u>)
non-count nouns	nouns impossible or difficult to count (Example: <u>*water*</u>, <u>*love*</u>, <u>*rice*</u>, <u>*fire*</u>)
object, direct	the focus of a verb's action (Example: I eat <u>*oranges.*</u>)
object pronoun	replaces the noun taking the action (Example: *Julia* is nice. I like <u>*her.*</u>)
passive voice	a sentence structure in which the subject of the sentence receives rather than performs the action (Example: The window <u>*was opened*</u>.)
past continuous	a verb form that expresses an action in progress at a specific time in the past (Example: I <u>*was reading*</u> a book at 8:00 last night.)
past tense	a verb form used to express an action or a state in the past (Example: You <u>*worked*</u> yesterday.)
period	a punctuation mark of a dot ending a sentence (.)
phrasal verb	a verb consisting of a verb plus an adverb or preposition(s), that has a meaning different from the words it is made up of (Example: <u>*call up*</u>, <u>*write down*</u>, <u>*run out of*</u>)
plural	indicating more than one (Example: *pencil<u>s</u>, child<u>ren</u>*)
possessive adjective	an adjective expressing possession (Example: <u>*our*</u> cat)
possessive pronoun	a word that takes the place of a noun and expresses ownership (Example: The hat is <u>*mine*</u>.)
preposition	a word that indicates relationship between objects (Example: The *pen* is <u>*on*</u> the *desk.*)

present perfect	a verb form that expresses a connection between the past and the present and that indicates indefinite past time, or continuing past time (Example: I _have lived_ in Paris. She _has worked_ here for three years.)
present perfect continuous	a verb form that focuses on the duration of an action that began in the past and continues to the present. (Example: I _have been waiting_ in line for an hour.)
present tense	a verb tense representing the current time, not past or future (Example: They _are_ at home right now.)
pronoun	a word used in place of a noun (Example: _Ted_ is 65. _He_ is retired.)
question form	to ask or look for an answer (Example: _Where is my book?_)
regular verb	verb with endings that are regular and follow the rule (Example: work = _work, works, worked, working_)
reported speech	a form of a sentence that reports on what was said or written by another person (Example: _He said he was sick._)
reporting verbs	a verb used to express what has been said or written (Example: She _said_ that she was leaving. He _complained_ that he was cold.)
sentence	a thought expressed in words, with a subject and verb (Example: _Julia works hard._)
short answer	a response to a _yes/no_ question, usually a subject pronoun and auxiliary verb (Example: _Yes, I am._ or _No, he doesn't._)
singular	one object (Example: _a cat_)
statement	a sentence or thought (Example: _The weather is rainy today._)
subject	the noun that does the action in a sentence (Example: _The gardener works_ here.)
subject pronoun	a pronoun that takes the place of a subject (Example: _John_ is a student. _He_ is smart.)
superlative	a form of an adjective, adverb, or noun that expresses the highest quality or degree of something (Example: _tallest, happiest, most comfortable, most beautiful_)
syllable	a part of a word as determined by vowel sounds and rhythm (Example: ta-_ble_)
tag questions	short informal questions that come at the end of sentences in speech (Example: You like soup, _don't you?_ They aren't hungry, _are they?_)
tense	the part of a verb that shows the past, present, or future time (Example: He _talked._)
transition word	a word that connects two sentences or paragraphs (Example: _first, next, then, lastly_)
verb	word describing an action or state (Example: The boys _walk_ to school. I _am_ tired.)
vowels	the letters _a, e, i, o, u,_ and sometimes _y_
_wh_- questions	questions that ask for information, usually starting with _Who, What, When, Where,_ or _Why._ (Example: _Where_ do you live?) _How_ is often included in this group.
yes/no questions	questions that ask for an affirmative or a negative answer (Example: _Are you happy?_)

► GRAMMAR REFERENCE

Frequency Adverbs	
Sentence	**Placement rule**
Luisa *often* goes running.	Before the main verb.
She is *usually* busy at weekends.	After the main verb *be*.
Yes, I *always* do. / No, he *usually* isn't.	Between subject and verb in short answers.
Note: *Rarely* and *never* are negative words. It is incorrect to use *not* and *never* in the same sentence.	

Clauses with *because*	
Sentence	**Rule**
My mother is very important to me *because* she taught me to be a good person.	When the *because* clause comes at the end of a sentence, no comma is needed.
Because my mother taught me to be a good person, she is very important to me.	When the *because* clause comes at the beginning of a sentence, use a comma.
My mother is very important to me *because* she taught me to be a good person.	Use a pronoun (e.g., *he, she, it, they*) to avoid repeating the subject noun.

To get something done				
Subject	***get***	**Object**	**Past participle**	**Sentence**
I	get	my hair	cut	I get my hair cut every month.
she	got	her clothes	cleaned	She got her clothes cleaned yesterday.

Comparative Forms of Adjectives				
	Adjective	**Comparative**	**Rule**	**Sentence**
Short adjectives	cheap	cheaper	Add *–er* to the end of the adjective.	Your computer was *cheaper* than my computer.
Long adjectives	expensive	more expensive	Add *more* before the adjective.	The new computer was *more expensive* than my old one.
Irregular adjectives	good bad	better worse	These adjectives are irregular.	The computer at school is *better* than this one.
Note: Remember to use *than* after a comparative adjective followed by a noun.				

Superlative Forms of Adjectives				
	Adjective	**Superlative**	**Rule**	**Sentence**
Short adjectives	cheap	the cheapest	Add *–est* to the end of the adjective.	Your computer is *the cheapest*.
Long adjectives	expensive	the most expensive	Add *most* before the adjective.	He bought *the most expensive* computer in the store.
Irregular adjectives	good bad	best worst	These adjectives are irregular.	The computers at school are *the best*.
Note: Always use *the* before a superlative adjective.				

Comparatives Using Nouns	
Our new apartment has *more bedrooms* than our old one. Our old apartment had *fewer bedrooms* than our new one.	Use *more* or *fewer* to compare count nouns.
Rachel's apartment gets *more light* than Pablo's apartment. Pablo's apartment gets *less light* than Rachel's apartment.	Use *more* or *less* to compare non-count nouns.

Superlatives Using Nouns	
Rachel's apartment has *the most bedrooms*. Phuong's apartment has *the fewest bedrooms*.	Use *the most* or *the fewest* for count nouns.
Rachel's apartment has *the most light*. Phuong's apartment has *the least light*.	Use *the most* or *the least* for non-count nouns.

Adverbial clauses with *before, after, when*

Sentence	Rule
After I returned the books, I stopped by the bank to make a deposit.	The action closest to *after* happened first. (First, I returned the books. Second, I went to the bank.)
Before I went grocery shopping, I stopped by the cleaners.	The action closest to *before* happened second. (First, I went to the cleaners. Second, I went grocery shopping.)
When everyone left the house, I made my list of errands and went out.	The action closest to *when* is completed and then the next action begins. (First, everyone left. Second, I made my list and went out.)

Note: You can reverse the two clauses and the meaning stays the same.
Use a comma if the adverbial clause is first.

Present Perfect

Subject	*have*	Past participle		Length of time	Sentence
I, you, we, they	have	been	sick	since Tuesday	I *have been* sick since Tuesday.
she, he, it	has	had	a backache	for two weeks	She *has had* a backache for two weeks.

Note: Use the present perfect for events starting in the past and continuing up to the present.

Infinitives and Gerunds after Verbs

Verb	Infinitive or gerund	Example sentence	Verbs following the same pattern
want	takes an infinitive (*to* + verb)	He wants *to get* a job.	plan, decide
enjoy	takes a gerund (verb + *ing*)	He enjoys *fixing* bicycles.	finish, give up
like	takes either	He likes *to talk.* / He likes *talking.*	love, hate

Gerunds/Nouns after Prepositions

Subject	Verb	Adjective	Preposition	Gerund / Noun	Sentence
I	am	good	at	calculating	I am good at *calculating.*
she	is	good	at	math	She is good at *math.*

Note: Some other examples of adjectives + prepositions are: *interested in, afraid of, tired of, bad at, worried about.*

Would rather plus Verb

Subject	*would rather*	Base form	*than*	Base form	Sentence
I, you, she, he, it, we, they	would ('d) rather	work alone	than	work with people	I would rather work alone than work with people.

Note: You can omit the second verb if it is the same as the first verb.
EXAMPLE: *I would rather work nights than (work) days.*

Possessive Adjectives and Pronouns

		Sentence	Rule
Possessive adjectives	my, your, his, her, our, their	This is *her* office.	*Possessive adjectives* show possession of an object and come before noun.
Possessive pronouns	mine, yours, his, hers, ours, theirs	This office is *hers.*	Possessive pronouns *show possession of an object and act as a noun.*

Comparing and Contrasting Ideas

Both Enrico and Liz <u>want</u> to increase the number of students in our class. *Neither* Suzanna nor Ali <u>wants</u> to increase the number of students in our class.	If two people share the same opinion, use *both . . . and* (+ plural verb) or *neither . . . nor* (+ singular verb).
Enrico agrees with bilingual education, *but* Liz doesn't. Ali doesn't agree with bilingual education; *however,* Suzanna does.	If two people don't share the same opinion, use *but* or *however.*

Punctuation note: Use a semi-colon (;) before and a comma (,) after *however.*

▶ IRREGULAR VERB FORMS

Base form	Simple past	Past participle	Base form	Simple past	Past participle
be	was, were	been	lend	lent	lent
become	became	became	lose	lost	lost
break	broke	broken	make	made	made
build	built	built	mean	meant	meant
buy	bought	bought	meet	met	met
catch	caught	caught	pay	paid	paid
choose	chose	chosen	put	put	put
come	came	come	read	read	read
do	did	done	ride	rode	ridden
drink	drank	drunk	run	ran	run
drive	drove	driven	say	said	said
eat	ate	eaten	sell	sold	sold
fall	fell	fallen	shake	shook	shaken
feel	felt	felt	show	showed	shown
fly	flew	flown	sit	sat	sat
forget	forgot	forgotten	sleep	slept	slept
find	found	found	speak	spoke	spoken
get	got	gotten	spend	spent	spent
give	gave	given	stand	stood	stood
go	went	gone	take	took	taken
hang	hung	hung	teach	taught	taught
have	had	had	tell	told	told
hear	heard	heard	think	thought	thought
hold	held	held	throw	threw	thrown
hurt	hurt	hurt	wake	woke	woken
keep	kept	kept	wear	wore	worn
know	knew	known	win	won	won
learn	learned	learned/learnt	write	wrote	written
leave	left	left			

▶ CONJUGATED VERB LIST

Regular verbs

Base: work **Infinitive:** to work

Simple present	**Present continuous**	**Simple past**	**Future**
I work	I am working	I worked	I will work
You work	You are working	You worked	You will work
We work	We are working	We worked	We will work
They work	They are working	They worked	They will work
He works	He is working	He worked	He will work
She works	She is working	She worked	She will work
It works	It is working	It worked	It will work

Present perfect	**Past continuous**	**Present perfect continuous**	
I have worked	I was working	I have been working	
You have worked	You were working	You have been working	
We have worked	We were working	We have been working	
They have worked	They were working	They have been working	
He has worked	He was working	He has been working	
She has worked	She was working	She has been working	
It has worked	It was working	It has been working	

Base: study **Infinitive:** to study

Simple present	**Present continuous**	**Simple past**	**Future**
I study	I am studying	I studied	I will study
You study	You are studying	You studied	You will study
We study	We are studying	We studied	We will study
They study	They are studying	They studied	They will study
He studies	He is studying	He studied	He will study
She studies	She is studying	She studied	She will study
It studies	It is studying	It studied	It will study

Present perfect	**Past continuous**	**Present perfect continuous**	
I have studied	I was studying	I have been studying	
You have studied	You were studying	You have been studying	
We have studied	We were studying	We have been studying	
They have studied	They were studying	They have been studying	
He has studied	He was studying	He has been studying	
She has studied	She was studying	She has been studying	
It has studied	It was studying	It has been studying	

Irregular verbs

Base: have   **Infinitive:** to have

Simple present	Present continuous	Simple past	Future
I have	I am having	I had	I will have
You have	You are having	You had	You will have
We have	We are having	We had	We will have
They have	They are having	They had	They will have
He has	He is having	He had	He will have
She has	She is having	She had	She will have
It has	It is having	It had	It will have

Present perfect	Past continuous	Present perfect continuous
I have had	I was having	I have been having
You have had	You were having	You have been having
We have had	We were having	We have been having
They have had	They were having	They have been having
He has had	He was having	He has been having
She has had	She was having	She has been having
It has had	It was having	It has been having

Base: run   **Infinitive:** to run

Simple present	Present continuous	Simple past	Future
I run	I am running	I ran	I will run
You run	You are running	You ran	You will run
We run	We are running	We ran	We will run
They run	They are running	They ran	They will run
He runs	He is running	He ran	He will run
She runs	She is running	She ran	She will run
It runs	It is running	It ran	It will run

Present perfect	Past continuous	Present perfect continuous
I have run	I was running	I have been running
You have run	You were running	You have been running
We have run	We were running	We have been running
They have run	They were running	They have been running
He has run	He was running	He has been running
She has run	She was running	She has been running
It has run	It was running	It has been running